Fact or Fiction?

Fortune-Telling

Other Titles in the Fact or Fiction? Series:

Fact or Fiction?

Fortune-Telling

Terry O'Neill, Book Editor

GREENHAVEN PRESS
An imprint of Thomson Gale, a part of The Thomson Corporation

THOMSON

GALE

Detroit • New York • San Francisco • New Haven, Conn. • Waterville, Maine • London

Christine Nasso, *Publisher*
Elizabeth Des Chenes, *Managing Editor*

© 2007 Thomson Gale, a part of The Thomson Corporation.

Thomson and Star logo are trademarks and Gale and Greenhaven Press are registered trademarks used herein under license.

For more information, contact:
Greenhaven Press
27500 Drake Rd.
Farmington Hills, MI 48331-3535
Or you can visit our Internet site at http://www.gale.com

Cover photograph reproduced by permission of The Cover Story/CORBIS.

ISBN-13: 978-0-7377-3508-6
ISBN-10: 0-7377-3508-2

Library of Congress Control Number: 2006935012

Printed in the United States of America
10 9 8 7 6 5 4 3 2 1

Contents

Foreword

Almost every one of us has experienced something that we thought seemed mysterious and unexplainable. For example, have you ever known that someone was going to call you just before the phone rang? Or perhaps you have had a dream about something that later came true. Some people think these occurrences are signs of the paranormal. Others explain them as merely coincidence.

As the examples above show, mysteries of the paranormal ("beyond the normal") are common. For example, most towns have at least one place where inhabitants believe ghosts live. People report seeing strange lights in the sky that they believe are the spaceships of visitors from other planets. And scientists have been working for decades to discover the truth about sightings of mysterious creatures like Bigfoot and the Loch Ness monster.

There are also mysteries of magic and miracles. The two often share a connection. Many forms of magical belief are tied to religious belief. For example, many of the rituals and beliefs of the voodoo religion are viewed by outsiders as magical practices. These include such things as the alleged Haitian voodoo practice of turning people into zombies (the walking dead).

There are mysteries of history—events and places that have been recorded in history but that we still have questions about today. For example, was the great King Arthur a real king or merely a legend? How, exactly, were the pyramids built? Historians continue to seek the answers to these questions.

Then, of course, there are mysteries of science. One such mystery is how humanity began. Although most scientists agree that it was through the long, slow process of evolution, not all scientists agree that indisputable proof has been found.

Subjects like these are fascinating, in part because we do not know the whole truth about them. They are mysteries. And they are controversial—people hold very strong and opposing views about them.

How we go about sifting through information on such topics is the subject of every book in the Greenhaven Press series Fact or Fiction? Each anthology includes articles that present the main ideas favoring and challenging a given topic. The editor collects such material from a variety of sources, including scientific research, eyewitness accounts, and government reports. In addition, a final chapter gives readers tools to analyze the articles they read. With these tools, readers can sift through the information presented in the articles by applying the methods of hypothetical reasoning. Examining these topics in this way adds a unique aspect to the Fact or Fiction? series. Hypothetical reasoning can be applied to any topic to allow a reader to become more analytical about the material he or she encounters. While such reasoning may not solve the mystery of who is right or who is wrong, it can help the reader separate valid from invalid evidence relating to all topics and can be especially helpful in analyzing material where people disagree.

Introduction

Fortune-telling is a term that covers a huge range of practices aimed at foretelling the future or revealing some other type of hidden knowledge that cannot be discerned by ordinary means, such as by reading, observing, or hearing. Other terms for *fortune-telling* include *divining, soothsaying,* and *prophesizing.* Weather forecasters, financial gurus, and sports bookies also predict the future, but their prognostications are based on statistics, history, and trends. In contrast, fortune-tellers' predictions are often considered to be magical, paranormal (beyond the normal), or supernatural.

Not everyone who consults a fortune-teller wants to know about the future: Sometimes people want to know better ways to deal with the here and now. Many consult fortune-tellers when they are worried or afraid of something. Others also consult fortune-tellers just for fun. The fortune might be a prediction about the future, insight into one's personality, a revelation about a momentous past event, guidance for making a decision, or some other kind of valuable information. Regardless of the motive for consulting a fortune-teller, the practice has existed since the earliest days of civilization.

Fortune-Telling in the Past

Fortune-telling is as old as humankind. Scientists who study ancient cultures have found plentiful evidence that fortune-tellers of various sorts have always played a role in society. In fact, many cultures revered dream interpreters and omen readers. The Old Testament of the Bible tells the story of Joseph, who interpreted the Egyptian pharaoh's dreams. Fortune-tellers influenced kings and military leaders as well as ordinary people.

Great monuments tell historians how vital astrology was to past civilizations. For example, many believe that Stonehenge in Great Britain, El Castillo temple in Chichén Ítza, Mexico, and even the Great Pyramid of Cheops in Egypt were all tools that ancient people used to gain information about the stars and planets to guide their lives.

Other artifacts also provide evidence of how important fortune-telling has been throughout history. For instance, in November 2005 a Chinese news agency reported the discovery of the oldest-known Chinese fortune-telling instruments, which were found in a prehistoric grave. Chinese archaeologists discovered a forty-four-hundred-year-old jade tortoise, consisting of a back shell and a belly shell containing several holes. A second tool, an oblong jade object about 4 inches (10 cm.) long and 2.5 inches (6.4 cm.) wide, with a pattern of broken lines carved into it, was found inside the tortoise shell. Gu Fang, a jade researcher and expert employed by the China Society of Cultural Relics, stated that the objects definitely did not have an everyday use and were most likely used in some kind of fortune-telling practice.

In the Western world, evidence of fortune-telling also dates back thousands of years. About three thousand years ago the Oracle of Delphi, one of the most famous fortune-tellers of all time, served the people of ancient Greece and had a major influence on the events of the times. The Oracle of Delphi was actually a succession of fortune-tellers (in this case, priestesses) who practiced their craft at a famous temple in Delphi. The place had a mystical fissure, or hole, considered by the people to be the center, or navel, of the earth. One ancient writer describes it this way: "In a dark and narrow recess of a cliff at Delphi there was a little open glade and in this a hole, or cleft in the earth, out of which blew a strong draft of air straight up and as if impelled by a wind, which filled the minds of poets with madness." The air entranced the oracle, or fortune-teller, enabling her to connect with the wisdom of the gods. Generations of Greeks from all over the land came to Delphi to consult with what they considered the great divine source.

Modern scholars have long dismissed the idea of the trance-inducing air currents as mythical. However, in 2001 a *New York Times* article reported that a group of scientists discovered that there may have been some truth to the story—at least as far as intoxicating air currents are concerned. They discovered that underground springs in that Greek region did produce several gases, including ethylene, which can cause altered mental states.

Famous Fortune-Tellers

There have been many famous prophets—another term for people who foretell the future, although it is usually applied to important religious figures such as Jesus Christ and Muhammad. The sixteenth century gave rise to one of the most famous secular, or nonreligious, prophets: Michel de Nostredame, better known as Nostradamus. Nostradamus was a French astrologer and physician. In his forties, he began writing a mysterious series of one hundred quatrains (four-line poems) that supposedly predicted events from his own time through the present. Reading his quatrains today, some people say that Nostradamus predicted World Wars I and II, the rise of Adolf Hitler, the assassination of U.S. president John F. Kennedy, and many other events. Those who believe that he did, indeed, achieve this amazing feat, point to specific lines in his verses that seem to apply amazingly well to current events. Those who are more skeptical say that his verses are written in vague terms that can be interpreted many ways. Whatever the truth, Nostradamus's reputation as one of history's great fortune-tellers will probably live on for many more years.

Fortune-Telling Today

Many people today dismiss fortune-telling as foolishness. However, a great number of others do subscribe to it. A 2005 Gallup poll revealed that nearly three-fourths of Americans believe in some aspect of the paranormal, including fortune-telling. Among other things, the poll results showed that 41 percent believe in extrasensory perception (the ability of people to perceive information with their mind alone, using the so-called sixth sense); 31 percent believe in telepathy (the ability to send and receive thoughts); 26 percent believe in clairvoyance (the ability to know the past and predict the future); 25 percent believe in astrology (the belief that the position of stars and planets affect one's life); and 21 percent believe that people can communicate with those who have died. All of these practices are related to fortune-telling, and such beliefs may be even stronger in other parts of the world. In some areas of Asia and Africa, for example, consulting fortune-tellers is a daily event for many people.

Fortune-telling today ranges from mere entertainment to serious matters. On the frivolous side, think of the horoscope found in most newspapers and many popular magazines as well as the fortune cookies delivered with the bill at a Chinese restaurant. Most people do not take these seriously, but it is hard to resist reading them and thinking about how they apply to one's life. Many young people have played with a "Magic 8 Ball" that answers any question asked with a profound "Yes," "No," or "Ask Again." In Japan the Noru Corporation produces a foaming bath ball that releases a numbered plastic ball as it dissolves in the tub; bathers can determine their fortune by comparing the number and color of the ball to a chart included in the package. In Korea some young people go to cafés that offer various types of fortune-telling along with the coffee.

On the more serious side, it is standard practice for large and small businesses in China to consult a feng shui expert, someone with knowledge about the best way to orient and furnish a building to ensure financial success. Feng shui is also becoming increasingly popular in the United States.

Popular Fortune-Telling Methods

There are literally thousands of ways people tell fortunes. Among the most familiar in North America are crystal-ball gazing, psychic reading, palmistry, astrology, tarot-card reading, tea-leaf reading, and dream interpretation.

Crystal-ball gazing. In crystal-ball gazing, also called *scrying,* the fortune-teller gazes into a clear crystal or glass ball or into another crystal-like or shiny, reflective surface (such as a bowl of water, a mirror, a pool of oil, or a highly polished black obsidian object). The fortune-teller sees images and interprets them to provide predictions and insights. Crystal-ball gazing has been known since ancient times, but some modern fortune-tellers use this method, too.

Psychic reading. Fortune-tellers who do psychic readings use various methods to tell a customer's fortunes. Among the most common methods are telemetry (handling an object belonging to the customer to gain hidden knowledge of that person), card reading, crystal-ball gazing, and mediumship (supposed communication with the dead).

Palmistry (cheiromancy). By examining the lines and ridges on a person's hand, the palmist is said to be able to provide information about relationships, health, and other matters.

Astrology (horoscopy). An astrologer studies the alignment of stars and planets at the time of the customer's birth—or at the time of a particular past or planned future event—to provide advice and information.

Tarot-card reading (cartomancy). Some fortune-tellers use plain playing cards, but many use tarot cards, a special kind of card deck laid out in specific patterns to gain hidden knowledge about a person's future or a particular situation.

Tea-leaf reading (tasseography). To tell a fortune with tea leaves, a person drinks a cup of tea made from loose tea leaves, not a tea bag. When just a bit of liquid is left, the customer or the fortune-teller swirls it around and carefully pours out the last liquid, leaving the tea leaves clumped in various patterns in the cup. The fortune-teller interprets these clumps and patterns.

Dream interpretation (oneiromancy). Everyone dreams, and some people believe that dreams tell them important things about their lives. The fortune-teller interprets the people, events, and items in dreams as symbols that reveal hidden knowledge.

Science and Fortune-Telling

There is very little scientific evidence—many scientists would say that there is *no* such evidence—that fortune-telling is a legitimate phenomenon. However, some modern efforts have been made to study some forms of fortune-telling scientifically. For example, beginning in the 1950s Michel Gauquelin, a French psychologist and statistician, conducted detailed statistical analyses to determine if people in certain occupations tended to be born under similar astrological influences. He discovered that athletes were disproportionately born under the sign of Mars, actors under Jupiter, and scientists under Saturn. Later analyses by other scientists were inconclusive, as some tests seemed to confirm Gauquelin's findings and others contradicted them.

Few scientists besides Gauquelin have attempted to conduct well-designed, controlled experiments of fortune-telling. In fact, most scientists declare fortune-telling to be a fraud. Yet people still believe. Author Ursula LeGuin writes in her novel *The Left Hand of Darkness*, "Legends of prediction are common throughout the whole Household of Man. Gods speak, spirits speak, computers speak. Oracular ambiguity or statistical probability provides loopholes, and discrepancies are expunged by faith." As LeGuin suggests, the bottom line is faith. Some people want to believe in the supernatural. In fact, people take all kinds of things on faith, including religion. Science does not yet have the answer to everything. Yet no one should blindly accept as true practices or beliefs that cannot be proven scientifically. You should give thoughtful consideration to what you choose to accept on faith. The articles in this book have been chosen to help you consider fortune-telling in a thoughtful manner; then you can decide whether fortune-telling is fact or fiction.

CHAPTER 1

Fact or Fiction?

The Evidence in Support of Fortune-Telling

Fortune-Telling Has Helped People for Thousands of Years

Raymond Buckland

Raymond Buckland has been studying, practicing, and writing about fortune-telling since 1964. His many books include Secrets of Gypsy Fortune-telling; Signs, Symbols, and Omens; Practical Candleburning Rituals; *and, as coauthor,* The Book of African Divination. *In the following selection, Buckland writes that people have practiced divination and fortune-telling since at least 4000* BC, *and that people have turned to fortune-telling practitioners out of fear, hope, desire, or simple curiosity all this time. Buckland argues that the practice would have died out long ago if it didn't work. He maintains, however, that just because a fortune-teller tells someone that something will happen does not mean that the prediction is set in stone; people have free will and can change their fortunes.*

The need to know what the future holds . . . most of us have that need at one time or another. Not necessarily simply wanting to know what horse will win a certain race, but desiring to glean at least an idea of where our lives are heading. The ability to divine the future is generally thought of as a gift. The very word *divine*—and its extension, *divination*—comes from "divinity," the belief that to be able to peer into the future is a gift of the gods. In many early civilizations, the diviner or soothsayer held a court position, with his or her utterances being sought for state matters and in cases of war and natural disasters.

Fortune-Telling Has Been Around for Eons

There is evidence that some form of fortune-telling was practiced in ancient China, Egypt, Babylonia, and Chaldea from at

Raymond Buckland, "Signs of Things to Come: An Introduction," *The Fortune-Telling Book: The Encyclopedia of Divination and Soothsaying.* Canton, MI: Visible Ink, 2004, pp. xi–xiii. Copyright 2004 by Visible Ink Press. Reproduced by permission.

least 4000 BCE. Divination, augury, and soothsaying all were part of everyday life in ancient Greece and Rome. The oracles at Delphi and elsewhere were freely consulted. Various forms of divination are mentioned throughout the Bible, in both the Old and the New Testaments. But seeking knowledge of the future almost certainly goes back much farther than any of these. Early humankind was undoubtedly anxious about the seasonal changes, about the success of the hunt, about fertility, and about the welfare of the coming harvest. By repeated observation over several generations of such things as weather, animal habits, and bird migration, such happenings were aligned with the later results to give the basics of prophetic lore.

The Roman statesman, writer, and philosopher Marcus Tullius Cicero (106–43 BCE) said that divination is a truly religious matter since it predisposes a belief in a deity that has arranged a destiny for all humankind. Pythagoras (c. sixth century BCE), the Greek philosopher, is known to have visited Egypt and parts of Asia, studying Magian and Chaldean lore; the so-called Pythagorean form of numerology is ascribed to him. Philosopher Aristotle (384–322 BCE) wrote a treatise on physiognomy. Plato (428–348 BCE) is credited with a belief in fortune-telling.

Fortune-Telling Is Found in All Cultures

Divination, or fortune-telling, is practiced in all cultures. What was once the prerogative of the shaman, and later became the jurisdiction of the priest, has today become the tool of anyone who has the inclination to try it. Tarot cards are read by all and sundry; astrological charts are cast and palms are scrutinized; crystal-gazers peer into the past, present, and future. For divination is not only the prediction of the future, but also the uncovering of secrets of the past and the present.

One of the earliest forms of divination was probably through dreams. Virtually everyone dreams, and many times a dream, on later reflection, turns out to have been a precursor of a coming event. From dreams, perhaps the path led to scrying—to gazing at a reflective surface and, through trance (light or deep), focusing onto events happening at a different time and place. Alongside these "internal" forms of divination are the "external" forms: observation of the actions of animals and birds, for example, and relating those actions to coming events. Other internal forms include automatic writing, use of pendula and dowsing rods, clairvoyance, cards, and tea leaves—all regarded as internal because their results depend upon sensory and motor automatisms and mental impressions. The external forms are dependent upon inference from external facts. Dice and other forms of sortilege, augury and omens, and casual meetings and overheard words are all beyond the immediate control of the diviner.

Why Fortune-Telling?

What induces people to turn to fortune-telling? It is usually fear, hope, or desire, along with simple curiosity. There is fear of future events not going the way you would like; fear of enemies, known or unknown; fear of illness, accident, hunger. There is also hope for what you desire. Many people also use divination for advice—to make an assessment of a career move or relocation, for example. A simple, daily card layout can smooth decision making. Much also has to do with an age-old belief that certain people are truly gifted with the ability to see the future, and then there is the desire to make use of their gifts. When the Romany, or Gypsies, first appeared in Europe in the fourteenth and fifteenth centuries, they found that they were looked upon as natural owners of such gifts. Persecuted as they were, the Roma did not hesitate to trade on any credulity of local populaces and to charge money to "tell the future." Over the centuries they did go on to develop true gifts for divination in many different forms. Even today Gypsies are viewed as specialists in this field.

The reason divination, or fortune-telling, has survived for so long is that it gives results. If it did not, it would have died out long ago. Obviously, individual results vary. This is also a field that is wide open to fraud. Yet despite the charlatans, there are innumerable instances of people learning of coming events and finding that what was prophesied actually came to pass. Many believe that certain people are truly gifted with the ability to see the future and desire to make use of their gifts. Documentation exists with a variety of professional societies, such as the (British) Society for Psychical Research, the American Society for Psychical Research, and the Parapsychology Foundation of New York, as well as at a large number of colleges and universities, including the Duke Parapsychology Laboratory in North Carolina, the University of Saskatchewan, the University of Leningrad, and the A.S. Popov Scientific Technical Society in Moscow. Records of Spiritualist churches and societies, of small home circles, and the evidence of tens of thousands of professional psychics and readers all lend credence to the fact that divination, fortune-telling, prophecy, or whatever label is applied, actually works.

We Can Affect Our Fortunes

Having said that, it must be emphasized that human life is not fatalistic. What is seen in "future readings," from astrological horoscopes to tarot-card spreads, is not written in stone. It is all no more than an indication of what is *likely* to happen, with the current forces at work around you, if nothing changes. But, of course, things do change, and it is within the power of the person whose fortune is being told to make change. If, from a reading, indications are that something negative is going to happen, then it behooves that individual to focus his or her attention on the turning events and ensure that the negative does *not* happen. Would this then show that the divination was incorrect, since it foretold one thing but now that has not come to pass? Not at all, for it foretold what was going to happen if things had continued as they were at the time of the reading. A later reading, taken during rapidly changing times, would have shown a different outcome.

Fortune-Telling Helps People Make Wise Decisions

Cassandra Eason

All people have something within that can guide their choices and future paths; using fortune-telling methods can help people tap into this powerful resource, writes Cassandra Eason, author of the following selection. Eason describes scientific research that some people think offers proof that, indeed, people do have "psychic and divinatory powers," or the ability to perceive and understand more than can be determined with the standard five senses. Once people have used fortune-telling techniques, Eason cautions, they cannot simply sit back and expect the predicted future to happen: they have to work with their inner powers to make the future happen the way they want it to.

Eason has written more than fifty books about psychic and supernatural experience, folklore, and superstition, including I Ching Divination for Today's Woman, Cassandra Eason's Complete Book of Tarot, *and* The Complete Guide to Psychic Development. *She has practiced various forms of fortune-telling for more than twenty years.*

> The intellect has little to do on the road to discovery. There comes a leap in consciousness, call it Intuition or what you will; the solution comes to you and you don't know how or why.
>
> —*Albert Einstein*

The wisdom that can be attained through casting runes, choosing tarot cards, or using any of the other "self-discovery" methods [regarded as fortune-telling] is timeless and beyond reason and logic. It is that of the divus, or god, within us all, sometimes described as the Higher or Evolved Self, whose knowledge is drawn from a pool of the experience of all humankind in all times and places, past, present, and future. The psychologist Carl Gustav Jung discussed the "two-million-year-old-man" contained in everyone—we can reach this repository of wise counsel through divination.

What Does Science Say?

Dr. Dean Radin at the University of Nevada, Las Vegas, has found startling evidence of the existence of psychic and divinatory powers. His telepathy experiments involved subjects who attempted to transmit one of four randomly selected images into the mind of someone in a sealed, soundproof room. By chance alone, it was estimated that the people guessing the projected images would on average pick out the correct image in one in four cases. Yet, in more than twenty-five hundred tightly controlled trials, Dr. Radin found an overall rate of accuracy better than one in three.

Telepathy is a thing of the present. What of the future? Dr. Radin also tested that most common kind of premonition: the sudden sense of impending doom that we have just before an accident or when we pick up an envelope and know—against all reason—that it contains bad news.

There is always a temptation to be wise after the event, and many people might say they had a feeling of unease before a tragedy even if they did not. So Dr. Radin decided to measure something that could not lie: the bodily reactions of his subjects. When we say that we "felt cold" just before an event or "felt a sinking in the stomach," we are not just using figures of speech. Unease can cause physiological changes. Our heart rate drops, we experience increased perspiration, and the pupils in our eyes dilate. Less noticeable but more easily measured are decreases in the electrical resistance of our skin and the volume of blood passing through our fingers.

Dr. Radin hypothesized that if people could really sense when they were about to have an emotional shock, it might be possible to detect these physiological changes a few instants before impact. His subjects were wired up, then placed in front of computer screens that were programmed to present a series of emotionally shocking scenes, mixed randomly with a much larger number of innocuous scenes of cheerful people and pleasant landscapes. He found that his subjects' physiological responses changed significantly for a shocking image, but remained flat for the innocuous ones.

What was unexpected was that the physiological changes appeared up to three seconds *before* the emotional images were shown, while the screen was still blank. This confirmed that the test subjects could sense the content of the next picture several seconds before it was shown.

Dr. Radin's research is described in his book *The Conscious Universe.* . . .

Fate can change anyone's life in an instant, through a lottery win, an unexpected promotion, a layoff, illness, or bereavement, or falling in love. Yet most examples of so-called fate are at least partly the results of our own or others' actions.

The Hand of Faith

For instance, you cannot win the lottery unless you buy a ticket, nor can you gain promotion unless another person leaves a post vacant by choice or a senior manager decides to create a new position. Even illness may be caused by a genetic or personal weakness or by the asocial habits of others.

What is more, our reaction to fate is crucial in deciding our future path, and sometimes there can be several options, which in turn affect future opportunities or obstacles in different ways.

Divination can reveal unconsidered paths and guide us to the best action or reaction, using the deeper knowledge that is out of conscious reach. These inspirational insights can be masked by a carefully formulated argument, expert advice, or the doubts and anxieties, guilt and obligations that can cloud decisions.

The Web of Fate

According to the Vikings, . . . our fate is not preordained but is determined by our own actions past and present—and those of our forebears who made us what we are. Each decision or action alters the pattern of the web of our personal fate that is constantly being woven. In the Norse tradition, the cosmic web of fate was created by the three Fates, or Norns, who were believed to oversee even the fortunes of the gods.

The first Norn is called Urdhr and speaks of the past, which influences not only our own present and future, but also that of our descendants. The second Norn, Verdhandi, tells of present deeds and influences, also strongly implicated in our future direction.

Skuld, the third Norn, talks of what will come to pass, given the intricate web of past and present interaction. Our future fate, or *orlog*, is constantly being changed as each new day adds to the web of interaction. The web is continually being torn apart and rewoven in ever more intricate patterns as the future becomes the present and ultimately the past.

How Divination Works

Divination is not a statistically accurate, mathematical method; it taps into the same instinctive processes that alert a mother to a child's danger even if her child is far away.

However, divination can take incredibly complicated forms. One reason for this is to give the intuition time to work, and for some people, following a long ritual can provide the time they need. Equally, the best inspirations sometimes occur in seconds, and if a method is too complex, the anxiety created can actually be counterproductive. If we accept, as Jung said,

25

that nothing occurs by chance, then every method, however simple, is really governed by synchronicity, or meaningful connections. This is how we end up with the "right cards," the right runes, or the right *I Ching* reading. It is a process of psychokinesis in which our unconscious knowledge influences the "fall of the dice." By the laws of the cosmos such information is provided in response to the individual's need to know an answer. This is why psychic gamblers are few and far between.

Asking the Right Questions

The hardest part of divination is asking the right questions. To demand certainties or precise timescales is to ignore the complexity of the future. It is also to disregard our own influence on our future or that of external circumstance and other people. . . .

Sometimes you may start with one question, but get an answer to an entirely different one (usually the question you needed to ask but had not realized or acknowledged). You can ask questions on any level and about any subject as long as the question is important to you or the person for whom you are asking, for need and emotion are the channels along which psychic energies flow most easily.

Sometimes there is no definite question or it is one that you cannot easily formulate. In this case, let the divinatory tools act as a focus for your unvoiced wishes and anxieties.

Fortune-Tellers Successfully Use Intuition and Revelation

Morwyn

The author of the following selection, Morwyn, wanted to find out what fortune-tellers or diviners believe about where their information about the past and future comes from. She sent surveys to five hundred professional diviners—generally referred to as psychics or channelers in this selection, which summarizes information from the 127 responses she received. The people quoted in the article are some of those who responded.

The survey responses showed that diviners hold a variety of beliefs about where the information revealed to them comes from. Some diviners believe their information comes from divine powers, some believe it comes from their own heightened intuition, and some believe it comes from spirit guides—disembodied spirits that communicate with them.

Morwyn is the pseudonym of Carolina daSilva, a Wiccan priest and ceremonial magician. She has studied traditions of magic and religion in many countries and has written several books relating to magic and the divinatory arts, including The Complete Book of Psychic Arts; Green Magic: The Healing Power of Herbs, Talismans, and Stones; Magic from Brazil; *and* Witch's Brew: Secrets of Scents.

> [T]he diviner put[s] aside his rational, logical, conscious mind and tap[s] into the larger, more spiritual, and—many believe collective—unconscious. It is that area of the mind where, if you will, "everything is known" and, therefore, knowable.
>
> —*Crawford Q. Kennedy, The Divination Handbook*[1]

Under my relentless prodding, a skeptic friend of mine who was having trouble with her love life went to see a local psychic. Sue was puzzled by her new lover's erratic behavior. Although he seemed to enjoy her company, periodically he lost interest in everything, including her. In her words, he "wound down like a clock." Then, as if by magic, he'd suddenly jump-start himself, and everything would be all right again.

She said nothing of this to the psychometrist [someone who divines information about another person by touching an object related to that person], who held Sue's glasses in her hand. After a few moments the woman told Sue that she was dating a man who used drugs in the secretive, lonely way many addicts abuse alcohol. The psychometrist could see the man locking himself in the bathroom and snorting cocaine. She also saw him driving a truck in the countryside and pulling off to the side of the road, sneaking a hit before meeting with a group of people whom he needed to direct in their work. She felt that drugs gave this reclusive individual the courage to be forceful.

"It's the same in his personal relationships," she said. "He needs the drugs to muster the energy to interact socially. He will never be happy with himself until he gets fed up with his dependence and banishes cocaine from his life."

The psychic assured Sue that the man would take steps toward this end within two years, but by then she would no longer be dating him. In a flash of insight, Sue realized that the psychic was right. She remembered all the times her lover dragged himself into the bathroom only to burst out the door a few minutes later, full of energy. She also knew that the psychic told the truth about the roadside pit stops because the man was a team leader in a corporation headquartered in the countryside outside of town, and that he drove his RV to work along lonely, rural roads. He complained a lot about having to deal with his "dysfunctional crew."

She was astounded at the psychometrist's insights. How could the woman, by holding her glasses, see and understand something about a third person's behavior, which despite Sue's intimacy with the man, she had not been able to figure out herself?

Soon after, the couple broke up. Two years later, Sue ran into her "ex" and he invited her to lunch. He confessed that he had suffered from long-term cocaine addiction that came to a head while they were dating, but that he was so much happier now that he had gone to drug counseling.

Intuition or Revelation?

What sources do psychics, as depicted in the above scene, tap to accurately zero in on details about character, relationships, and future events, and how do they contact these sources? Some believe that psychics and channelers commune with heavenly powers and that the information they transmit is divine revelation. Others claim that the source of "divinity" is found within; while still others conceive of it as intuition, which can be developed like any skill. So, is it really intuition, a supposed inherent faculty that everyone possesses, or are some people gifted by divine powers and receive messages through revelation?

The psychics in the survey disagree on this point, which is at the heart of all issues related to the paranormal. When asked, "How large a role does intuition (versus pure psychic revelation) play in your readings?", thirteen (mostly channelers) answer "none," seven declare that it is "all" intuition, seventeen claim that intuition plays "a large role," and two indicate a "small role." Several respond in percentages, with fifteen indicating that they feel that revelations and intuition are evenly divided. Twenty-five do not distinguish between the two. One reader asserts that her mood and her client's needs and expectations determine which she uses. Another clairvoyant says that "it's about 75% intuition and 25% common sense, good advice, educated guesses, and real knowing."

Evidently the topic of intuition versus revelation is a hot issue in the psychic community. This is seen in the responses to the survey. Respondents tend to divide into one camp or another and express diametrically opposed views with an enthusiasm bordering on vehemence like the following:

> All intuitive feelings are the right brain beginning to pick up, so all are psychic! Your understanding of psychic is vague! ([Irene] Hughes, presumably referring to intuition, which is a right-brain function.)

> I consider intuition and the psychic much the same thing. Perhaps the psychic is developing the intuition. ([Connie Marie] O'Very)

> Without intuition one could not be psychic. ([Robert A.] Ferguson)

> All people have intuition but what I have are psychic revelations—visions—that come to pass. ([Patricia] Mischell)

Sue Burton-Hidalgo sums up the topic with this eloquent statement:

> This is a great question: I am delighted someone recognizes the difference. I'd say my sessions are sometimes more intuition, and sometimes more divine revelation, but most often it's about 70% intuition/30% revelation. After reading professionally for so many people for so many years I actually have to "say no" to my intuition in order to attune to revelation.

[Patricia] Hayes offers another thoughtful insight when she explains that "psychic ability is trained, intuitive sensitivity. Psychic revelations are usually given for a specific purpose," thereby implying that they both can happen to the same person.

[Jean Ann] Fitzgerald puts it like this: "Intuition gives daily life information while revelation speaks of universal truths. Something can be revealed about daily life, but the purpose is to demonstrate universal truths."

The Effect of the Astral Plane*

In the hot topic, "Is it intuition or psychic revelation?" question, I use the term "psychic revelation" instead of "divine revelation" because not all psychics and channelers who believe in an external source for their information feel that the information originates with Divinity. William E. Butler, noted parapsychologist and one time head of the magickal order Servants of the Light, recognized the importance of intuition in developing ESP [extrasensory perception], but pointed to a kind of astral clairvoyance whereby the psychic tunes into "apparently living beings who have no physical body."[2] He tells how people of all ages and cultures have believed in these beings as a source of knowledge about this world, and have called them by many names—the devas of the Orient, dryads and oreads of ancient Greece, the Lordly Ones of Celtic times, angels, fairy folk, and elemental spirits.

These "spirits," Butler posits, may actually represent consciousnesses that have acquired existences via the concentration of thoughts and emotions of people over the centuries, and inhabit what is known as the astral world. "This great world of the astral," Butler comments, "is well named the World of Illusion. At the same time, the illusions are in the artificially created appearances of that world; in itself it is as real as any other realm of nature."[3]

According to psychical researcher Willis F. Whitehead,[4] telepaths and sensitives share a sympathetic bond with the astral world and find it easier than the rest of us to communicate with "those who live in the celestial infinitude," in other

---

* The astral plane is a dimension beyond the physical, a place where spirits exist who can be messengers between the divine and earthly realms.

words, non-physical intelligences who dwell in the "astral flame," as he calls this plane of existence. Whitehead likens the astral flame to a sun that radiates thoughts in the form of light. The psychic becomes a kind of solar collector of these light-thoughts from the "Exalted Ones."

Theosophists take a different view, and see the "astral light" not so much as a group of intelligences, but as a gigantic record book where all thoughts, emotions, and events throughout time are imprinted. Since they do not conceive of time as a linear series of events, all future thoughts, emotions, and events (as well as those of the past and present) are recorded in [this gigantic record book called] the Akashic records. They believe that psychics possess the "key" to this "diary," and are able to open it up and "read" about events as remote in the past as the life and times of King Tut, as personal and immediate as whom Aunt Tillie is going to marry, and as all-encompassing as the impact of nuclear energy on the twenty-first century world's environment.

Spiritualists believe that this information comes from spirits of the dead residing on the astral plane, who have made a commitment in their lives on the Other Side to help people who are still earthbound to improve their lives.

Who's in Control?

When asked, "Do you have a control or spirit guide that helps you with readings?", respondents answer 2:1 that they do (64% say "yes;" 32% say "no"). Those on the "yes" side name anywhere from one to a dozen spirits with whom they maintain contact. Often they conceive of the entities as protective forces that shield them while they are in altered states. Here are representative replies about spirit guides:

> [Yes, I communicate with guides:] a Hispanic man, a Mayan or Aztec warrior who is a protector and guide, a female ancestor, and a higher being from the cosmos. ([Lee] Lewis)

A man from Atlantis and a gypsy Arab for protection. I believe it is better for a psychic to have a control. (Joy)

Though I have many guides, Asonji . . . protects me when I'm in an altered state. ([Sarasvati] Boyet)

Some readers are aware of a directing force in a more general way. Three say that while they can't see the entities, they know that they are there to guide them.

"I am aware of a collective (versus individual) up there heightening my energies," affirms [Jennifer] Shepherd. "There is an energy that connects me to the 'all;' universal energies. I have no name for it; it encases me and opens my chakras [force centers] to tap into other people's souls." states Ginger.

Respondents speak of being surrounded by entities, but see them as personal guides, not necessarily to be called forth to aid readings. Ina Rae relates, "At first I was not aware of a guide, but she spoke to me constantly, giving me advice, and answers to my questions and problems. She's a blessing to me, but not essential to readings."

[Morris] Fonte agrees. "Mother Mary gives me guidance and brings me close to God, but not every psychic needs a guide."

[Martha C.] Lawrence remarks that she channeled an entity for a while, but found it unsatisfactory after a time. "I grew beyond him."

Respondents like Hughes find the idea of a control distasteful. She claims:

In mediumship, sometimes there is a special entity that comes to "open the door" for others to be able to talk with me—but any psychic/medium who claims to have a "control" or "lots of guides" is not psychic but I believe they really want to talk about "how many" guides know them and "control" them. No one controls me. No entity should be a "control" of your brain! Again, it is the ability of the right brain to "see" and to pick up and to hear!

An anonymous respondent shares the sentiments, "No, I don't want a control! I am a solitary soul. I don't want to share the inner space at all."

[Kurt] Leland, a channeler, elaborates:

> The information comes to me from Charles [the entity he channels] in the form of energy or images. I do not think of Charles as a personality, but more like the call letters of a radio station or the log-on password of a computer system. When I first began to channel, I was told "there is a sound that will help you gain access to the clearest possible information." That sound, a kind of meditation mantra, was not a word I knew, but it resembled the name "Charles."

> Later, when asked who "he" was, Charles gave a different answer every time. This brought me to the realization that I could never verify who or what the source of the information was, but could only vouch for its positive effects on the lives of other people. As a consequence of the experience, I tend not to trust channeled entities with flashy pedigrees—I think that (some channelers do this) to compensate for a low level of self-worth . . . or sometimes a high degree of skepticism.

When it comes to teaching psychic self-development classes, practitioners remain divided. "I do not encourage my students to develop a control," [Nancy F.] Myer affirms. "I believe that leads to more errors, and less responsibility is taken for what is said . . . Don't use Red Feather [the name of a controlling entity] as an excuse when you're wrong. Just apologize. . . . No human is ever 100% accurate."

On the other hand, Burton-Hidalgo, who does have a control that filters information to lessen the impact on her because she is too "empathetic and tender-hearted," disagrees. She maintains that:

> [A] control is not necessary, but useful [when I am channeling] for large groups of 100 or more. A control manages the karmic resonances of the crowd so that I do not become sidetracked by deeper emotional or spiritual agendas.

When I teach channeling courses, I introduce beginners to a control. I call it the "gatekeeper." I find this reassures the students that they have someone to share the responsibility/ability to "get information." It also sets up a system to make sure negative or astral energies stay off of them.

The Message in the Medium

All these comments that show differing points of view about how psychics receive their information may cause you to wonder whether the data transmitted by paranormal means is just a figment of the practitioner's imagination. This would be a premature conclusion to draw because you need to consider that psychics may obtain their knowledge in different ways.

Butler sheds light on how this works. He believes that psychic information travels through the body by way of two different nerve pathways, the involuntary nervous system and the cerebro-spinal system. In the first case, the images, though clearly seen, are not clearly understood. The vision may also not be under the control of the will of the person who is experiencing it:

> Often when it is needed it cannot be brought into action, and at other times, when it is not required, it breaks through into the waking consciousness. The other mode of working, through the voluntary [cerebro-spinal] nervous system, has the advantage of being under the control of the psychic, and can be aroused at will. It is also far less dependent upon what, in psychic experimentation, are known as "conditions."[5]

Since the perception of how and where the person receives information differs, perhaps it also feels different to each individual, thereby leading psychics to conclude that the sources are different, as well.

Notes

1. Crawford Q. Kennedy, *The Diviner's Handbook* (New York: New American Library, 1989), p. 10.

2. William E. Butler, *How to Read the Aura, Practice Psychometry, Telepathy and Clairvoyance* (1968, 1971, 1975; reprint, New York: Destiny Books, 1978), p. 31.
3. Butler, p. 33.
4. Willis F. Whitehead, "Occultism Simplified," in *Keys to the Occult: Two Guides to Hidden Wisdom* (North Hollywood: Newcastle Publishing Company, 1977), p. 27.
5. Butler, p. 18.

Fortune-Telling Is an Ancient Science

Jenni Kosarin

Jenni Kosarin, the author of the following article, argues that fortune-tellers, like Wall Street stockbrokers and weather forecasters, analyze patterns and trends to determine what the future will hold. Some fortune-tellers analyze the way a set of cards is laid out when dealt in a special manner; others analyze a series of coin tosses (in an ancient Chinese fortune-telling method known as I Ching); still others analyze patterns of lines on a person's hand. Just as Wall Street brokers' and weather forecasters' predictions sometimes change, so does the future the fortune-teller predicts for a client. Kosarin explains why predictions change and describes how to approach fortune-telling with common sense.

Kosarin has been studying and practicing fortune-telling methods for more than fifteen years. She is the president of the American Psychic and Tarocchi (tarot cards) Society in Florence, Italy.

You enter an old psychic shop and see a mysterious "gypsy" woman with jangling bracelets, hoop earrings, and a multicolor turban. Lights from the candles flicker around her, casting curious shadows. You think you see a black cat sitting beside her. You smell jasmine incense and something musty.

Suddenly, the woman speaks. "Come closer!" You move closer, albeit with a bit of uncertainty. "Tell me. Tell me what you want to know," she whispers huskily. "Madame Bovart will now tell you everything you want to know." And with a pass of a hand over her crystal ball, she begins. Can she really see into your future?

Jenni Kosarin, *The Everything Divining the Future Book*. Avon, MA: Adams Media, 2003, pp. xi–7. Copyright © 2003 Adams Media Corporation. Reproduced by permission.

Divination Is Ancient

Since the beginning of time, people have always been fascinated by the idea of seeing into the future. Though it may seem far-fetched, we do it all the time. Wall Street brokers do it every day as they try to predict the movement of the market. All of us in our daily lives analyze patterns and trends that help us make predictions as to what the future holds. And that's what fortunetelling is all about. Through analyzing patterns and trends, ancient signs and symbols, we're able to get a glimpse of the future. There is one big difference, though. Divination has been around a lot longer than Wall Street.

In fact, divination has existed since before recorded time. It can be traced back more than 30,000 years. Shamanism, for example, is one of the oldest practices of divination. It originated in Siberia and the Far East, and spread to North America, where it is still practiced by Native Americans. The art involves talking to spirits and interpreting the sounds and movements of animals.

Another ancient method of divination, numerology, was developed in the Mediterranean region and was shaped by Pythagoras, a Greek philosopher and mathematician (sixth century BC). Ancient Chinese divination, on the other hand, was derived from tradition, philosophy, and science, through the wisdom of oracular judgments of the I Ching (The Book of Changes) some 3,000 years ago. And many believe that Tarot was influenced by the mystical Hebrew teachings of the Kabbalah. (For instance, Kabbalah is based on the twenty-two paths and the Tarot consists of twenty-two Major Arcana [mystic scenes].) Ancient Persian divination tools ranged from the use of omens to palmistry. And the Northern Europeans developed an alphabet of runes, which the Nordic people used for writing and divination as far back as 100 BC.

Seeing Life's Possibilities

Divination evolved throughout the ages with the help of magicians and psychics, but philosophers and scientists were also very much involved. For example, ancient Greek philosophers Plato and Socrates were adherents of Pythagorean principles. And the work of Sigmund Freud made leaps and bounds in helping us look into the subconscious mind as well as the hidden intricacies of sleep and dreaming. Carl Gustav Jung, at one time associated with Freud, wrote and analyzed the role of "meaningful coincidence" and how it was to be applied to our lives. He believed that life events do not happen by chance, but by the merging of time, matter, space, thought, and spirit. Essentially, this means that coincidences, according to Jung, really do have higher meaning.

Divination allows you to see all of the possibilities of life, and forces you to live life to the fullest. There is an old Sanskrit proverb from a famous [Hindu] swami [monk] named Vivekananda, who said: "It is the coward and the fool who says 'This is fate.' But it is the strong man who stands up and says 'I will make my fate.'" Facing your fate is what the art of divination is really about. And who wouldn't love to know what's going to happen in the next few weeks, months, or years? . . .

Fate and Predetermined Destiny

Is our destiny predetermined? Yes and no. You do have a life lesson that you need to learn in this lifetime. However, the path you choose to get to that knowledge is up to you—and the possibilities along the way are infinite.

Choice and free will always exist in life, and you should never look to divination for set facts. What divination *can* do is show you the possibilities and offer you the guidance you might need for the future. Think of divination as a friend or a mentor. In the end, the way you choose to live your life is up to you.

What do you choose to make your reality? If you have your cards read and the Tarot card reader tells you that you'll meet your love in four months' time, are you going to sit home every night, watching television and waiting for the phone to ring? Of course not. Sure, it's possible that you could meet that person after a year, by chance, in an elevator or on the subway, but why wait? Good things won't happen unless you're ready for them. For example, if someone tells you that you will be famous one day and you take no steps to advance your career, what can you expect? Get ready, get set, and get out there!

Also, remember to take everything with a grain of salt. If you're worried about your health, don't go to a psychic in order to find out what's wrong. One woman had a small lump in her breast and asked a psychic about it. The psychic told her not to worry, that it was nothing, benign; so she never went to the doctor to have it checked. Later it was confirmed to be cancerous. Always get a second opinion and never go to a psychic for medical advice. That's what doctors are for!

Finding Your Path

Eventually, you will learn your lesson and you will experience what you need to, and your experience will enhance and strengthen your soul and your purpose—your reason for being here. Everyone has a life purpose. What would happen if we were all Einsteins or Mozarts? We'd have a whole lot of people doing physics and writing music, but no one to actually implement the scientific theories or perform the musical pieces.

Everyone has a role in the world and contributes to the workings of the universe, so that it continues to exist in harmony. Granted, our world doesn't always seem very harmonious—there is still a lot of pain and suffering caused by wars, conflicts, diseases, and natural disasters. That is why it is so important to know what your role is in the world, so that you can make it a better place in which to live. The key is to figure out where you want to go and how you're going to get there.

Once you know, divination can be a great tool to help nudge you forward in the right direction.

To give you a very basic example of destiny and predisposition, let's take your teeth. That's right—your teeth. You can brush your teeth five times a day and floss like a maniac, but you may still get cavities. Why? It may be that you are genetically predisposed to cavities. On the other hand, there are a few people who don't take care of their teeth and yet hardly ever have any problems—not even a single cavity in their entire lifetime. Why do these people have fewer cavities when the rest of us have a mouth full of them, though we brush and floss regularly? Science can give you a more detailed explanation as to which hereditary traits might contribute to having healthy teeth, but the point of the matter is, some people have them and some people don't—it's something you were born with. Can we say that you are predestined to have healthy or unhealthy teeth? In a way, yes, we can.

And if it is true that some of us were born with good teeth while others were born with a photographic memory, and still others have great musical ability—and, in fact, so far scientists have not found a genetic explanation for these types of traits—isn't it possible that each and every one of us is born with a specific destiny in mind?

Is Divination for Real?

Of course, scientists will argue until they're blue in the face that if something can't be proven, it's simply not valid. This may be true. But even today, in the twenty-first century (and with all our scientific research), not all the questions have been answered. No one can tell us when an earthquake will happen. They can only tell us (again, from patterns and study) where it is likely to eventually happen. Divination, in the same way, relies on belief, faith, and research. It resembles science because it is also a method derived from recognized patterns and studies done throughout history.

But how do we know it's real? We just do. There are many cynics who doubt the possibility of peering into the future and seeing what's going to happen. But a good psychic does not claim to be able to see the future as if it is set in stone. What he can do is look at the momentous, life-changing events such as a major career change or a second marriage you were destined for—events that will happen in your life if they're meant to happen.

If you want proof, look around you. Some of us were born into this lifetime with extraordinary luck with certain things. Others will suffer constantly in love; still others will become famous; and a number of us will live, contentedly or not, our normal, routine life, going to work and coming home to our families every day. But everyone—rich or poor, outgoing or shy, happy or not so happy—will learn the things they need to learn to fulfill their destiny.

People who are skeptics of how divination is done always ask the same questions. For instance: "If I have my Tarot cards read every day, it will say something different. How can all of it be true?" Well, you should never have your Tarot cards read every day—once a month or every couple of months is sufficient.

How often you should rely on divination depends on the method you use. For instance, you can use numerology and crystals (when used for meditation or healing) every day. I Ching can help you solve everyday problems as well as those that are life-affecting. Runes can steer you in the right direction for small questions or for meditation, but should not be consulted every day. You also should not use a crystal ball daily, because it is meant only for scrying (tapping into the future). Palmistry provides a general guide to your character, your personality, and your life destiny, but because the lines of your hands will not quickly change their shapes, you should not use this method very often.

Back to the Question

The reason the Tarot cards can change what they say every day is because everything you do in your life changes your possibilities for the future. For instance, you go to a psychic Tarot card reader and she tells you that your career is going well and you will have the opportunity for advancement in about three months. The next day you have a tiff with your supervisor or you say something to rub a colleague the wrong way. This little scene can alter your near future.

Does that mean that you should steer clear of everyone and watch every small move you make? Sit behind your desk and worry? Of course not. This is simply how fate operates. Sometimes it's not even up to you. It could be something as simple as the director of human resources receiving a letter from the head of the company, unbeknownst to you, saying that there is no money in the budget right now to promote even the more deserving of candidates.

The key to living with your destiny is to avoid excessive worrying and not try to control it. Controlling and manipulating your destiny is the surest way to land flat on your face. You'll still have to learn your lessons. And it might just be more difficult for you. Be kind to yourself. Search for help when you need it. And don't try to stifle your suffering—feel it and live it so you can continue on, learn, and live a happier life. If you constantly avoid it, it will eventually find you anyway. This is what we sometimes call "karma."

In Buddhism, karma is the idea that "what goes around comes around"—that your fate and your future are determined by your past. If you lived your past life by the rules of the universe and were kind and helpful to others, you are rewarded in your next life. If you did not, your next life is more difficult.

Karma

The Buddhist view of karma assumes that our present positions in life are the result of justice and retribution. Some

Western philosophers say that the Eastern view of karma helps those in power, who can pat themselves on the back for having good karma. In Western teachings, karma is more about cause and effect within a particular lifetime and does not require belief in reincarnation. It is the energy around you, at this moment or period in time. If you spread the good energy through good deeds, it will come back to you—it's like catching a good wave if you're surfing, it works for the little things in life, like having the instinct to pick a winning number, meeting and connecting with a person who might help you in the future, performing a presentation well on a certain day, and so on. Of course, karma is not foolproof—anyone can have a bad day. Sometimes, it has more to do with your destiny than with the details of everyday life.

The best thing you can do to make your destiny work for you is to be good to yourself and to the people around you, and to pace yourself—indulge sometimes and cut back other times. Search for friendships, work, and play that bring out the best in you. Your karmic lessons will find you in this lifetime and teach you the things you need to know.

The Bias Against Fortune-Telling Is Unfounded

J. Rainsnow

In some communities fortune-tellers are able to operate freely, without regulation. In others, fortune-telling is legal as long as the fortune-teller has an official city or state permit. In yet others, fortune-telling for money is strictly against the law. It is this latter group that concerns J. Rainsnow, author of the following selection. Rainsnow argues that a major reason fortune-telling is illegal in so many places is that the authorities are concerned about fraudulent fortune-tellers bilking people out of money. Rainsnow concedes that while there are, indeed, fraudulent fortune-tellers, he believes that most are genuine and sincere and provide help to people who need it. He notes that it is unfair to treat all fortune-tellers as though they are con artists.

J. Rainsnow maintains a Web site, www.rainsnow.org, that promotes spiritual development. He is the author of several books, including The Journey of Rainsnow: One Man's Past-Life Journey—A World's Future *and* The Message of Rainsnow: A Spiritual and Cultural Vision for Beginning to Save the Earth.

Divination, at its best, is a highly valuable and spiritual endeavor, not only bringing useful information to Humanity, but increasing our connection to the Divine (for a sacred state is achieved during the seeking, receiving, and transmission of this material). Much of the traditional bias of our mainstream religions against divination comes, not from its "unholiness," but from the fact that much of the religious and state power of "antagonistic civilizations" was intertwined with it, and symbolized by it. (Reference is frequently made to

J. Rainsnow, "A Note on Fortune-Telling and the Law," www.rainsnow.org. Reproduced by permission.

the magicians, soothsayers, and "wise men" of the alien, "other," or enemy cultures: [for example, in the Bible] to the magicians of the Pharaoh—Exodus 7—or the astrologers and sorcerers of Nebuchadnezzar—Daniel 2. While the Greeks and Romans had their interpreters of signs and omens.) The bias against divination was, as far as I can tell, far more than just an effort to make contact with the Divine more direct, by eliminating the fetish/pseudo-iconic role of divining objects (which, properly used, however, do not thwart, but facilitate, communication with the Divine); it was really, in my opinion—at its root—an effort to break free of the shadow of the "oppressors," symbolized by foreign kings and warriors, and state priests and magicians. Bondage in Egypt, the Babylonian Captivity, later the crucifixion of Christ and persecution of Christians by the Romans—who had their own occult power structure, embodied in the college of pontifices, the college of augurs, and a network of "foreign" haruspices [fortune tellers]—most likely left a very negative impression upon the hearts of the ancient Hebrews and the early Christians. . . . It is very likely that the oppressed Hebrews and Christians came to resent the way in which the religious institutions of Egypt, Babylon, and Rome collaborated in their repression; and that they came to despise many of the rituals and practices of these institutions as characteristics or tools of the enemy. Divination, so important in these powerful and dominating ancient cultures, may have become as hateful to the Hebrews and the Christians as the Nazi eagle, the Nazi swastika, and the Iron Cross became to the conquered peoples in Europe, during WWII: not things harmful, in and of themselves, but infuriating because of what they were associated with. (In other words, the power and usefulness of these mystical forms of searching and finding—which could be utilized by corrupt as well as by moral people—may have been rejected by our civilization's spiritual ancestors due to specific cultural and historical associations, and due to prejudices created by negative historical experiences—not due to any inherent fault in the concept of divination. Just the same as a man robbed or beaten by an individual of another race might unjustly develop a racist bias against that entire race, the good along with the bad, so diviners—the priests and advisers of oppressive kings in a crucial formative period of our Western cultural history—may still be suffering from the "bad publicity" of days gone by. It is a shame, since divination, outside of our own religious tradition, has been a nearly universal aspect of spirituality across the globe, significant not only to the ancient Egyptians, Babylonians and Romans, but also to Native Americans and Hawaiians, to African and Asian cultures, and to most European societies before the arrival of Christianity.)

A Growing Bias Against Divination

As time went on, this initial bias against divination as "something the bad guys do," may have become exacerbated by the Christian Church's efforts to crush the competition of rival spiritual belief systems, in an effort to hoard all "spiritual power" (authority) for itself. What was spiritual, and did not come from it—what was spiritual, and could be gained outside of it—was, therefore, not only rejected, but demonized. "If it doesn't come from us (God as we represent Him), then it must come from The Devil." This monstrously polarized view of the Universe, overlooking the simple fact that Spiritual Truth can be found and related to in many different ways, was a terrible blow against human unity. For it made spirituality not a common meeting ground of all people, but a point of division, in which particulars overshadowed essence. In effect, the Christian Church sought to acquire "sole rights" to spirituality on the earth, and to drive every other religion out of town. It was a power grab, pure and simple, and during the Middle Ages it led to massacres and expulsions of Jews (they were "blamed" for the Bubonic Plague, attacked, ghettoized, and also exiled from many lands); the slaughter of Muslims

(Jerusalem was captured by the Crusaders in a blood bath the equal of any war crime); the annihilation of out-of-favor Christian sects (the Cathars of southern France had their towns and castles stormed by force, and the Eastern Orthodox Christians of Byzantium, likewise, saw their city sacked); the torture, imprisonment, and execution of many individuals of all walks of life by the Holy Inquisition, and other councils of religious conformity (Galileo and [Giordano] Bruno stand out); and the burning of pre-Christian loyalists (pagans), who were only attempting to remain true to their old faith. The spiritual wealth of these old religions was brushed aside, and their followers were called "devil-worshippers"—which is rather like calling someone you do not like a "child molester," something terrible that will poison people's minds against him, discredit him, and set him up for your attack. . . .

The point, here, is . . . that there has been a tendency for religious institutions and belief-systems, in the past, to seek "territorial expansion," acquiring new minds, just as nations acquire new lands. That when these movements of expansion cannot proceed peacefully—resisted, perhaps, by a powerful, alternative belief-system—they have often been pushed forward by means of propaganda, intimidation, violence, and repression. In the process, many spiritual treasures may have been taken away from us, and many vibrant spiritual facets painted black, and placed off-limits, with the goal of reducing the rainbow of our souls to but one color—the color of the winners of the religious war. In my mind, there is no doubt that the fundamentalist Christian bias against divination which is evident today, is the result of exactly one such historical process.

Of course, divination is alive and well in our modern society, in spite of all this, although it is frequently harassed, and misunderstood. Indeed, it is a central component of the New Age, which is, on the whole, very friendly towards original forms and concepts of Christianity, rooted in Christ's own teachings and example of love. . . .

The Negative Stereotype of the Fortune-Teller

What is really generating the most trouble for "fortune-telling," divination, and other esoteric arts, today, is probably the charge of fraud. The bias of conservative elements of Christianity, and the skepticism of secular society, are not really enough to drive "fortune-telling" off the streets, even when they combine their efforts (odd bedfellows that they are), to do so. This is due to the First Amendment protections of the Constitution. However, once the charge of fraud is leveled, then the landscape changes, and the battle seems to shift from being one of ideological/metaphysical confrontation, in which the rights of the diviner "to be different" are constitutionally protected, to one of "consumer protection," in which the rights of the consumer (to be defended from fraud) seem to empower the government to crack down on the "fortune-teller."

Of course, the negative image of the fortune-teller, generated by centuries of religious and cultural bias against him, does not provide him with a good starting point to face this new challenge. And then, there is the power of the scientific model of reality, which many secular enforcers of justice have internalized. According to this model of reality, which they accept as absolute truth, the ability claimed by the "fortune-teller"—whether it is to be able to divine the future through the position of the stars, the spread of the tarot cards, or images glimpsed in a crystal ball—is just not possible! Therefore, in claiming to be able to know something of the future in this way, the "fortune-teller" is already guilty of fraud! Like a man who comes up to you and offers to sell you the Brooklyn Bridge for $100, he is charging money for something that he is unable to deliver. In other words, taking your money for nothing. "Ripping off the consumer." . . .

This prejudice, sometimes rooted in powerful places, puts the "fortune-teller" in a bad spot, right away. Just by practicing his art, he may be considered to be a criminal, because his art is off the map of the people who have the power to judge him. . . .

Besides the initial prejudices in our society, which endanger the work of the modern-day diviner, there is, unfortunately, also a long legacy of abuse and fraud in this "profession," which adds to the negative stereotype the "fortune-teller" must endure, and which fuels the tendency of mainstream society to distrust him, and to imagine the worst about his work. . . .

At the Mercy of the Law

Whereas there is no doubt that there is, indeed, a time and place for the legal prosecution and restriction of certain unethical practitioners of the esoteric arts, it is equally clear that the esoteric arts, as a whole, should not have to pay the price for what some unethical members, or infiltrators, of the occult/New Age community are doing. Modern medicine has not been illegalized or banned because of the unethical and incompetent actions of some of its doctors. Nor have law enforcement agencies been outlawed, due to the abuses committed by some members of their community. Likewise, priests and ministers have been found guilty of embezzlement, misuse of funds, even rape, yet the religious institutions of which they are a part have not been threatened with illegalization due to these personal transgressions. In this way, the world of the esoteric arts should not be targeted due to the transgressions of some individuals. Those individuals should be targeted.

Today, although esoteric arts such as astrology, tarot card reading, psychic reading, palm reading, rune-stone casting, and spiritualism flourish in America, they often do so in a cramped space of legal ambiguity, harassment, and occasional prosecution. "Anti-fortune-telling" laws remain on the books in many localities, and though they are mostly not enforced, the threat of enforcement limits the space and ways in which the esoteric arts may operate. In theory, laws like this—unenforced laws on the books—ought to provide authorities with a tool for dealing with extreme abuses, while letting everyone else alone: just like vagrancy and loitering laws, which provide a legal "excuse" to prosecute potentially dangerous characters who have committed no serious crime, while leaving everyone else alone. But the truth is, "anti-fortune-telling" laws, which are most always vague and sweeping, place the community of the esoteric arts at the mercy of the local governments, which have the tools they need to prosecute, harass, and prohibit them whenever they wish. It may not be a question of a transgression committed, but of which way the wind is blowing; a matter of local politics, scoring brownie points with conservative cultural elements, overreacting to fear generated by misperceptions and ignorance. Practitioners of the esoteric arts, therefore, desire to see these laws struck from the books. They would like to see their work treated in the same way as any other form of work, held to clear and well-defined standards of responsibility, but not singled out to be especially vulnerable just because of the minority metaphysical orientation which underlies it.

In the effort to address this issue, some practitioners of the esoteric arts have not only sought to lobby government institutions to get "anti-fortune-telling" laws off of the books (and to prevent new laws from being written); for some time, they have also been seeking to generate a case which will make it to the Supreme Court, and solve the problem once and for all, at the national level. However, in most cases where prosecutions have occurred, the charges have been dismissed by local judges, leaving the diviners free, and nullifying the local "anti-fortune-telling" laws, but leaving such laws intact in other cities, counties, and localities. (Only by losing a case at the local level, and working their way up through a series of appeals cases, could the "occultists" get their case to the Supreme Court, where the issue could be dealt with in one blow, from the top. . . .

I wholeheartedly endorse the liberation of the esoteric arts from the inappropriate legal mechanisms set up to repress them. In a "free society," people must be free to have their own spiritual beliefs, their own view of reality; and if they believe that it is possible to catch glimpses of the future, and to see into the secrets of the human soul, why should they be prevented from using what is within their reach, in a constructive and compassionate way, to help improve the lives of others, and to make this a better world for us all?

Coffee Grounds Can Reveal the Future

Sophia

Some fortune-tellers read tea leaves to make predictions about the future. Less common in North America, but just as ancient a practice as tea-leaf reading, is the art of fortune-telling using coffee grounds. The author of the following selection, Sophia, reports that people have been reading coffee grounds since at least AD 1000. Sophia describes how she learned to read coffee grounds when she was a child. She notes that she learned to use her imagination to tap into her intuition, but to be very careful to separate fantasy from fact. By following these practices, she became very skilled at divining people's futures.

Sophia is the professional name of Rebecca Sargent, a professional psychic and spiritual teacher. She teaches seminars on such topics as fortune-telling with cards, reading coffee grounds and tea leaves, and psychic development. She has written several books, including Fortune in a Coffee Cup, Fortunetelling with Playing Cards, The Little Book of Love Spells, *and* Hex the Ex.

Although reading coffee grounds to learn about the present or future sounds like a new gimmick, it really isn't. By "reading," I mean viewing the coffee grounds in a person's cup after they have finished drinking it, and using one's psychic abilities to *see* images and omens in the patterns the leftover grounds make. No one knows how old the practice of reading grounds really is, but a conservative estimate puts its origin around AD 1000. The use of coffee itself as a beverage is older and seems to have originated in Ethiopia. From there it was brought to Europe by Arabian traders, and eventually spread

Sophia, *Fortune in a Coffee Cup: Divination with Coffee Grounds.* St. Paul, MN: Llewellyn Worldwide, 1999, pp. 3–13. Copyright © 1999 by Sophia. Reproduced by permission.

around the world. Coffee ground readings themselves probably evolved soon after the medicinal and recreational use of coffee was discovered. What likely happened long ago is that the power of coffee was recognized in the spiritual traditions of the area, and its use for divination quickly became part of these traditions.

Coffee ground readings are still popular in the Middle East, Northern Africa, and in the other countries along the Mediterranean seacoast. Even today you will see people involved in readings on the streets in those places. I have seen fortunetellers plying their trade in the local markets and in coffee shops or outdoor cafes, revealing what the future holds for their clients. The art of giving coffee ground readings is passed down by an oral tradition—I have not been able to locate any books or articles on the subject. The tradition, I've been told by my grandparents, was spread slowly around the world by the Gypsies. From Africa to Europe to America, in a roundabout way, this is how it came to me.

Psychic Skills Passed Down from Family

The wonderful, interesting, and accurate art of coffee ground reading was passed on to me in the small city of Aberdeen, Washington, when I was just a toddler. My grandparents, native Northwesterners, were fortunetellers who spent their time giving readings to others, counseling them, and telling them their future. They were very involved, I later discovered, in the spiritualist movement of the 1920s, which is a whole other story. My grandfather was born with a veil or caul, a thin extra skin appearing over the head of a newborn baby. It is said to be the mark of second sight, or psychic ability. If the veil is pulled off from the back, the psychic will be able to see the past and if it is pulled off from the front, the psychic will be able to see the future. My grandfather's veil was pulled off from the front—he was an excellent psychic and could see the future easily, or so people said. He was an experienced and sought-out psychic, and I was told that I inherited my gift from him.

I was not born with a veil, but I do have a widow's peak, which by our tradition indicates the same thing, though a veil indicates a much more intense ability and is a rarer phenomenon. As I grew up, I learned from my family many kinds of divination arts—telling fortunes with playing cards, reading tea leaves, and scrying with crystal balls. Later, I became proficient at direct psychic readings and I also learned how to be a medium. This all started when I was three years old!

Reading coffee grounds was the first method of fortune-telling that I learned, at the same time as I learned how to read letters. Some people learn about local history, some learn cooking, and some learn how to play the piano; my family taught me to read coffee grounds for others. My younger sister and I spent many hours at my grandparents' home learning how to read the grounds. Though my grandmother was also a well-versed psychic, my grandfather was my primary teacher. He told me that he learned to read the grounds from the gypsies when he was a boy, at the turn of the [twentieth] century.

My great-grandfather deserted his family, and my grandfather, along with his other family members, moved out to the country and sometimes picked crops in order to make a living. The family later moved into a run-down home near a Gypsy camp—Gypsies did the same kind of work. My grandfather was outgoing, loving, and very funny. His bedroom window overlooked a meadow were there was a permanent Gypsy camp and their music and laughter put him to sleep at night.

He told us that the most beautiful sound he ever heard was the Gypsy king playing the violin at night around their campfire. My grandfather learned to play the violin from this man, and was likewise very impressed by the psychic talents of these people with whom he made friends. As he became closer to them, the king's mother and an older Gypsy woman in the camp taught him divination.

Coffee Tastes Best

Of the many types of divination my grandfather learned, his favorite was coffee ground reading. He always said that the main reasons were that coffee just tasted better then anything else and that it was so easy and so accurate. Tea leaf reading, he felt, was not as good, though it was and still is obviously more popular. I tend to agree. Coffee grounds just seem to give better information than the leaves. When talking of this, he would say that if you want to know the past, present, or future, then look into a cup of coffee and you will find the answer.

This is as true today as it was a thousand years ago. Cups of coffee hold a lot of information that is easy to pick up. It is very easy to do, once you get the knack of it.

Seeing with the Inner Eye

I asked my grandfather how it worked, and he told me, "Just look at the grounds left in the empty cup as if they were clouds in the sky." When you lie on your back and look at clouds, you can see so many different shapes, and they are always shifting. They can be anything your imagination wants to make them. A cloud could be a house or an apple. It does not matter what it *really* looks like—what you see with your inner eye is what matters. Everything that you see in an empty cup streaked with coffee grounds has a meaning. Everything resembles a symbol, and you must take those symbols, translate them, and weave them into meaning with the help of your inner vision.

What makes readings personal and helps the reader pick up on things is that the people who are about to get a reading carefully drink the coffee first, while thinking about their questions. That makes it *their* coffee and *their* fortune. I was taught that the essence of the person is left in the cup, and the reader must then convey the meaning and practical information left there to the person.

My family would often sit around a stove on typically rainy Northwest days. My sister and I would be given cups of coffee, no bigger than doll cups, to which we would add a pinch of extra grounds to make more interesting readings. My grandfather would drink out of his big white cup and then slowly turn the cup counterclockwise three times, all the time concentrating on what his questions would be or what his desires were. He would then wait for the last of the coffee to drip out. He would finally pick up his cup and begin to read, while we sat fascinated and entranced.

As we asked questions or he explained key points, we would remember them and later apply them to our own little doll-cup readings. He would often coach us or correct us. We loved our coffee cups and they seemed to hold all the mysteries of the universe. My grandfather was not only a very good and kind man, he was also incredibly accurate with his readings and often predicted things no one could have known. Because of his modest fame in our small coastal city, he was a popular person to visit. This began to affect my life as well.

My grandfather once said to me that he was counting on me to learn how to read the grounds and be better then anyone. I took his advice seriously, and when his friends dropped by to have their fortunes read, as they often did, I would be the first person to do it. I was the *warm-up* reader before my grandfather gave them the serious reading, and so I, a little child, would look into their cups to see what their fortunes were. I had a natural talent for this and soon I was being requested for readings. My grandparents treated this art as a very spiritual thing, not as a game. They felt that to be a psychic was a gift from God, and taught me to never take my powers for granted. My grandfather said that, like any such gift, it must be shared and treasured and never forgotten. Never use it lightly, he cautioned me, or for entertainment. As my grandparents got older, they stopped telling fortunes so much. My grandfather said that it was harder for him and made him feel sad to *see* so many things that were problems for others.

Like any activity, the more you do it, the better you get at it, and this was a pleasure for me. I still love to give readings and I feel that I am improving at it.

One day a man came to get his fortune read and my grandmother introduced him to me as: "the man who always had work during the depression." Joe would stop by to see if we needed anything, and he always had something to give us, usually a sack of apples or a loaf of freshly baked bread. My grandparents never asked a fee for readings, it was against their spiritualist beliefs, but everyone knew that you should give something for a reading—it was implied. Usually a form of barter is what happened.

Sorting Fact from Fantasy

One time, when Joe came, my grandfather said, "Try the granddaughter out, she's learning and she is pretty good at what she does." He would drink the coffee in my grandparents' company and I would go outside to play or walk across the street to see the neighbors' horses until I was called back into the little house to read the grounds. I loved the special attention, but I did not want the responsibility that I was being compelled to shoulder. I guess it was like anything that you are not sure about in the beginning, I looked at these things as mystic chores. Later I learned that it was a service that I could do to help others so they could make decisions about what they needed. Joe was very respectful of me and what I had to say. The difficult part for me as a kid was to sort out fact from fantasy—that is, what it was that I needed to concentrate on. This is still the key skill, to find the best way to look at the psychic picture *as a whole*. It was difficult when I was young because I had to think, "what can I, a kid, say to a grownup that will make sense?"

Joe was a simple man, so I could explain to him what I saw in my own terms and this was okay with him. One day when I was looking in his cup, I saw the number "2" at the top of the cup—that meant two hours, and it was near a $ sign and a bird. I interpreted these simple symbols for him. He would get good news soon that would involve money. Joe thanked me and left. Later that afternoon he called to tell us that he had received a letter with $200 in it. Apparently he had overpaid his taxes and the money was a refund! These kinds of coincidences happened regularly after readings. It wasn't strange to me at all, and no one told me that it was unusual.

As time went by, I became more accurate in my readings and grasped the complexities more completely. I started giving readings to my girlfriends. I liked doing readings when my subject and I had more in common. I was especially good at picking up on their boyfriends' names, and if they had a future together or not. One girlfriend was in love with a man whose initials were L.O. These initials never did appear in her cup, but another man's did—the initials J.D., with a ring next to them. The location of the initials indicated that it was somebody in my friend's future, and the ring meant that it would be a serious relationship. We knew everybody in town and we could not figure out who J.D. could be. He turned out to be an older man outside of our circle of friends and he did marry my friend sometime later. They are still married. The husband does not believe us about this reading, but we love to tease him about it.

Often it seems that details I pick up don't mean anything at the time, but later they turn out to be right on. What you *expect* doesn't matter; what is important is the design of the grounds and what you *see*. I was taught it is necessary to always be honest and tell people what you see. I did then and I continue to do so today.

Fact or Fiction?

CHAPTER 2

The Evidence Against Fortune-Telling

Fortune-Telling Is a Sham

Katy Yocum

At psychic fairs, psychics and fortune-tellers use various tools, including tarot cards, tea leaves, and crystal balls to tell people about their future. Usually, such fairs also feature booths from which vendors sell books, crystals, and other things related to the psychic world. In this selection reporter Katy Yocum describes a psychic fair she attended in Louisville, Kentucky.

Yocum went to a booth for a reading with a graphologist, someone who analyzes a client's personality or makes predictions about their future based on characteristics of their handwriting. The graphologist asked Yocum to write a question on a piece of paper, presumably to get a handwriting sample. However, it appears to Yocum that this was just a way for the fortune-teller to get clues about her concerns or interests that required no psychic ability. Yocum writes that her experience at the psychic fair was highly unconvincing and that the fortune the graphologist told her was no more insightful than statements any ordinary person could have provided.

Yocum has degrees in journalism and creative writing and writes feature articles for Louisville Magazine.

I was nervous, I admit it, as I sat down with the woman who would predict my future.

She didn't seem to sense my trepidation. Her soft-fleshed face was expressionless, and her eyes wandered vaguely from place to place. A redhead somewhere in late middle age, she seemed passive, even serene.

As for myself, I felt like squirming. What was I doing here, surrounded by astrologers and tarot-card readers in a semi-dingy Ramada Inn conference room? I'd come to this psychic

Katy Yocum, "A Reading Between the Lines," *Louisville Magazine*, July 2001, pp. 1–5. Reproduced by permission of the author.

fair on a lark, as a little oddball entertainment. But now I was starting to regret it. It seemed a little seedy, like taking tips from a shady-looking regular at the track or paying for one of those adult movies on a hotel TV. And another thing: I value my privacy. What was I thinking, paying a stranger to peer into the nooks and crannies of my personal life?

The worst part of it was, if this woman lived up to her literature, she could read me like a book. She knew how many Chips Ahoy I'd had before bed the previous night. She was probably tsk-tsking at how much I'd paid for those cute sandals at Dillard's. And if my nerves were jangling at the thought of my past being exposed—well, that was nothing compared to the idea of unveiling my future. I wouldn't even know what to be embarrassed about.

I was actually relieved when she misread my name off the appointment card. "Kathy?" she asked. "Katy," I corrected her, feeling perversely cheered by her mistake. Apparently she wasn't omniscient after all.

"Write a Few Words"

"Here," she said, pushing a sheet of stationery and a pen toward me, past a small statue of a white-bearded wizard. "Write down a question for me. It don't matter what you write."

Around us, a few casually dressed attendees conferred with other clairvoyants and astrologers. Others examined the crystals, books and miscellaneous wares that lined the room's perimeter. Well, I'd already committed to paying for this. I might as well go through with it. I wrote a few words across the top of the page. Then I slid the paper back toward her and watched her impassive face as she read my question.

I was new at this, but I imagined the question I asked could make or break the reading. A psychic could really make hay from a good, juicy query—something like "Does my boss know about that 50,000 bucks I embezzled?" or, "When is that no-good sumbitch husband of mine coming home?" Me, I went the generic route: "What does the next year hold for me?" If this woman was going to pocket my $20, she was going to earn it. I wasn't handing out any gratuitous hints.

As it turned out, a gratuitous hint or two might have been in order. Either her psychic powers were getting a cold start that day or else my future was just plain muddy. Instead of launching out with predictions, vague or otherwise, she began barraging me with questions: What did I do for a living? Was I married? How old were my husband and I? Any kids? I felt mildly offended. If she were really a psychic, shouldn't she sense those things?

Inane Blather

But that, it turned out, was just the warm-up. What followed were the most amazing predictions, the most stunning insights—oh, wait; that's the way it happens on TV. But this wasn't Miss Cleo's Psychic Hotline; this was the Ramada Inn. And what actually followed was the most inane blather, the most stultifying career advice imaginable. "Write down 10 things you think you might like to do," she intoned, staring into the middle distance. "Then narrow it down to five. Then. . ."

As she droned on, I began to wonder why this woman was bombing so badly. Maybe being in a roomful of psychics had overloaded her circuits. Maybe I was blocking her powers with my desire for privacy. Or maybe—just maybe—some sort of psychic polarity had reversed itself. Her psychic skills had clearly abandoned her; what was to say they weren't channeling themselves through me? Why, of course! It made perfect sense!

Suddenly I could see this woman's life. It was all coming clear. I sensed a home in Indiana (oh, wait, I saw that in her literature). I saw people filing into her home for psychic readings. I sensed cash exchanging hands. Something about unreported income . . . but then the vibrations got fainter.

Ding! A little alarm bell went off, and my first and only psychic reading limped across the finish line. Just like that, my $20 bill floated straight out of my future and into hers.

A Valuable Lesson

I left the fair that day 20 bucks poorer, but I'd learned a valuable lesson. For the first time, I could understand the appeal of this line of work: You could absolutely slink as a psychic and it just wouldn't matter. This woman could have read me her grocery list and still charged me for the reading. After all, who's to say cabbage and macaroni-and-cheese don't figure into my future? And then it hit me: Maybe I should try my hand at this psychic business.

Since then, I've been working to develop my skills. In fact, allow me to give a small demonstration right now. You there, reading this article! Come closer . . . closer . . . I'm sensing something. My powers tell me you are a successful professional sort of person . . . or perhaps you're married to one . . . or perhaps you're sitting in the waiting room of a successful professional person as you read this.

But there's more. I sense that you are a person of culture. You enjoy the arts, dining out. You have a favorite little eatery in the Highlands or perhaps on Frankfort Avenue. You have money in the stock market, but it hasn't done so well this past year or so. Yet you're planning to do some traveling this summer, probably before the Labor Day weekend. Ah, yes, the vibrations are strong with you.

Well, what do you think? I hope you enjoyed your reading. But if you didn't, just remember—the psychic energies, they come and go.

Either way, don't forget to pop that 20 bucks in the mail to me, care of *Louisville Magazine*. The sooner you mail it in, I sense, the brighter your future will be.

Tarot Cards Cannot Reveal the Future

Mark Patrick Hederman

Some people with strong religious beliefs think that people who practice fortune-telling—or who go to fortune-tellers—are usurping God's rights and may even accidentally allow evil into the world. Some argue that Ouija boards, tarot cards, and other tools of the fortune-teller should be banned. Mark Patrick Hederman, however, is a Catholic monk and philosopher who does not believe that tarot cards are evil; in fact, he believes they can be very useful tools for meditating and tapping into one's unconscious. In this selection, Hederman writes that although tarot cards are useful in helping people gain self-knowledge, they do not foretell the future and do not have any magical power that allows someone to see what is to come.

Hederman lives in Ireland and is a founding editor of the Irish cultural journal The Crane Bag *and the author of* The Haunted Inkwell: Art and Our Future, *and* Kissing the Dark: Connecting with the Unconscious.

We live our lives in a tiny area of light, as if we were huddled under a sub-standard streetlamp. This small circle of visibility that surrounds us is what we call conscious life. We live and move in our day-to-day world within this orbit. But there is a vast area of darkness and of mystery beyond this floodlit patch. This outer darkness is what we call the unconscious.

The unconscious is that area of ourselves that is beyond the reach of our ordinary ability to reason, outside the realm of our day-to-day activity. It is a distinct area. As such it is vast, strange, hidden. We would hardly know it was there if we did not get inklings of it, whispers, rumours. That is why we have to use images from our familiar world to describe it. . . .

Seeking Spiritual Attunement

Towards the end of the nineteenth century and the first half of the twentieth century, resistance to entry and discovery of the unconscious was particularly trenchant and totalitarian. Most fundamentalist movements in society were versions of religious thought systems, all of which waged war against art, for instance, as a kind of idolatry, whose purposes were presumed to be hedonist if not evil. The discovery of the unconscious by scientists and doctors was condemned as immoral, and all attempts to understand the reality of humanity as a bodily phenomenon were resisted as degradation of our true nobility as spiritual creatures of God.

One significant symptom of such a mind-set is the attitude to that most primal and expressive form of art which is dancing. After three years in Africa I am aware of how irretrievably impoverished most of us Westerners have become in this essentially human way of being. Dance is the manifestation of the spirituality of matter, demonstrating the most elegant and spiritual poise of our nature in its bodily aspect. It is both the accomplishment and the expression of well-being and the most fundamental and artistic way of attuning ourselves to the rhythm of the universe. It has been part of religious self-expression in most cultures the world over. It is the most natural way to participate in the liturgy, for instance. But in our religious education there is an endemic prejudice against it. Africans who have been trained in our religious ceremonies have in a few years not only lost their natural aptitude for it but have learned to despise it as an irreligious activity. . . .

The tarot cards, as well as teaching us to dance mentally, also provide us with an easier route to the unconscious. This alternative route uses some of the materials, shapes, signs and symbols used by artists and our dreams. Playing with the cards in a certain way helps us to cover the same area, using similar symbols and shapes, but in a more accessible and less daunting way. The tarot cards introduce us to a new kind of space and another kind of time. The space involved requires from us a kind of lateral vision; the time involved is experienced as coincidence, more professionally labelled synchronicity, another Greek word. The major arcana [mystic scenes on the first twenty-two cards] of the tarot are visual aids to the unconscious. They are vivid shorthand portraits, something akin to the Chinese ideograph or picture writing. These latter do not try to represent a sound, as other alphabets or musical annotations do; they abbreviate a person or a thing. The ideogram for 'sun' or for 'tree' in the more primitive Chinese alphabets is an outline sketch of these two realities; so much so that certain artists claim to be able to see these references immediately without having learnt the language. In a similar way, the pictures on the tarot cards are recognisable to all of us; they can be used as a visual slide-rule on which we can play out our own particular psychological equations.

Window to an Alternative World

Like the stained glass windows in Chartres [a Gothic cathedral in France], the tarot cards bring us back to a time before what we call the modern way of thinking started. They provide a window to an alternative world, another way of thinking. They are relics of a religious sensibility. Like secret agents in disguise they have been hidden as entertainment and as fortune tellers' gimmicks, but as such they are camouflage for a secret army.

Between the mystery and the structures we have received as Church, Scripture, Tradition, there is an abiding testimony to the time before these were set in place. Such testimony was, of necessity, oral or visual, pre-literal stimuli. The tarot trump cards are 22 spiritual exercises through which we can immerse ourselves in the spirit of that living tradition. This requires an activity different from and deeper than academic study or intellectual explanation. Deep and intimate layers of the soul become active and bear fruit when we meditate on the arcana of the tarot. The cards are something like a ferment or an enzyme (Greek: *en* = in, *zeume* = yeast) which can stimulate the spiritual and psychic life. What they reveal are not secrets (things hidden deliberately by some human will) but *arcana*, which means what is necessary to know in order to be fruitful in the domain of spiritual life. In Latin, *arca* is the word for a chest; *arcere* the verb means to close or to shut. In English the word 'arcane' comes from this root. It means something secret or mysterious. The word is also used in such well-known artefacts as Noah's ark and the ark of the Covenant in the Hebrew Bible.

So, we can visit the 22 cards as if they were an art gallery. These trump cards also act as projection holders, hooks to catch the imagination. They represent symbolically those instinctual forces operating autonomously in the depths of the human psyche which [Swiss psychiatrist Carl G.] Jung called the archetypes. It is from this unconscious part of ourselves that our relationship with the spiritual and the divine emanates, as does every other aspect of our relational being. The cards can be useful to us in either our vertical or our horizontal relationships. They can help to negotiate our passage through the world of the spirit as well as the world of other people.

Projection is an unconscious, autonomous process whereby we see in persons, objects and happenings in our environment those tendencies, characteristics, potentials, and shortcomings that really belong to ourselves. Every child is born with these hereditary projectiles; there is nothing we can do about it. But we can become aware of what we are doing at all times, and we can sketch out for ourselves the wardrobe or the cast that we are continuously projecting. . . .

Tarot Cards Cannot Foretell the Future

People are alarmed, amazed, convinced, by the accuracy with which their futures can be outlined and their personalities sketched by so-called experts who read the tarot cards. Let us begin with a statement of fact: Anyone who tells you what the future is going to be is telling you a lie. There is no future laid out like a map. The future is what we make it. Of course, we can be told, and some are better than others at surmising what is most likely to happen if we go on being the way we are, and others around us do likewise. The tarot cards cannot foretell the future. No one can foretell the future. It doesn't take a genius to know that people are going to die, fall in love, make fortunes, split up, move houses, change jobs, in every month of the new century. People who predict such things have no vision of what is about to happen, they know that you are a human being, they sense your personality, they absorb your psychic energy, some more sensitively than others, and they 'prophesy' about your future. Whatever they say that has no relevance or doesn't come to pass is forgotten; anything that rings true, or that corresponds to what happens to you later, is often exaggerated and afforded significance out of all proportion.

These cards are evocative images, or symbols, which portray in archetypal form an inner reality that is common to all of us as human beings, and yet peculiar to each of us at every moment of our lives. This is why they can be used to 'predict' what is about to happen to us. There is a limited number of things which can happen to any or every human being in the course of any or every day of our lives: we are going to meet someone 'significant' (who isn't? Every person we meet is potentially our 'significant other'); we are going to meet up with death in some shape or form; we are going to achieve some goal; we are going to 'fall in love'; we are going to have an accident; we are going to come in for some good/bad fortune. But when these inevitabilities have been predicted, they suddenly take on the aura of prophecy, especially when aligned with the particular unfolding of our ordinary lives. The normal becomes paranormal because it has been pointed out as predestination. People we meet are enlarged and invested with significance; our amorous impulses are primed and ready to greet the next post-person [mail carrier] who knocks at the door. The music of what happens becomes the orchestrated fanfare of the wedding, funeral or prize-giving march, which we have prerecorded, with original variations on the well-worn theme, courtesy of our psychic.

The future can only be shaped from whatever already exists, from the fairly predictable set of options which each one of us is.

Fortune-Tellers Are Crooks

May Chow

Many people who do not believe that fortune-tellers can predict anyone's future think that they are nevertheless essentially harmless people and that going to a fortune-teller is akin to participating in a party game. But others argue that fortune-tellers are not so innocent. One of the biggest complaints about fortune-tellers is that they bilk some of their clients out of money—in some cases, many thousands of dollars. This is one reason many cities and states outlaw fortune-telling altogether.

In the following selection, author May Chow describes a fortune-teller in San Francisco, California, who cost her client $15,000 in just three months. Chow describes how Mrs. Sonia, the fortune-teller, was able to gain influence over her client and take advantage of her. Chow also applauds efforts by the police in San Francisco and other cities who are trying to stop this kind of fraud.

May Chow is a staff writer for Asian Week, *a newsmagazine published in San Francisco.*

Nestled away in the shaded alleyway of San Francisco's upscale Maiden Lane, in a space that now houses an art gallery, once stood a place of mystery and clairvoyance. For $20, Mrs. Sonia promised any person who set afoot in her quaint store the possibility of love and romance, health and happiness. But it was all in the cards.

Mrs. Sonia was not a matchmaker, therapist or doctor. She was a fortuneteller. [In the early nineties], she operated her business out of this modest store. Now long gone without a trace, she has left behind heartache and a criminal investigation.

May Chow, "Psychic Scams," *Asian Week*, April 25, 2003, pp. 1–9. Reproduced by permission.

Lisa* is a victim of Mrs. Sonia, and it was only after a decade of keeping her silence that she came forward to authorities. In a period of three months, she was swindled out of more than $15,000. Now, she is working with the San Francisco Police Department (SFPD) to track down Mrs. Sonia, and teaming up with the Board of Supervisors and the District Attorney's Office to propose a law that would require the city's fortunetellers to hold permits.

An Innocent Beginning

One day back in 1991, as Lisa was window-shopping around Maiden Lane, a little boy jumped out and handed her a flier advertising Mrs. Sonia's services.

The slip of paper, with the word "fortuneteller" scribbled in Chinese, caught the attention of Lisa, who at the time was a recent graduate of UC Berkeley and like all her single friends, trying to find a decent date in the city.

"My friends and I always talked about having someone tall, dark and handsome enter our lives, so I thought that I'd go in for a reading on my love life just for fun and see if a good boyfriend was in my future," says Lisa, 37, who is Chinese American. "I never intended it to be anything serious or true. I saw it as just entertainment."

With the flier in her hand, Lisa slipped into the dim room where Mrs. Sonia sat, tucked away amongst the curls of incense smoke, flickering candles and dark, velvet curtains. She went in with a smile and curiosity on her face, reminding herself to be skeptical but at the same time, open-minded.

Mrs. Sonia looked Lisa up and down, and invited her to have a seat at the small, round table. The soothsayer immediately took out a deck of tarot cards and shuffled them, all the while darting glances at Lisa.

* Name has been changed to protect anonymity.

"I'd never had a tarot card reading done on me before, this was the first time," Lisa says. "I didn't know what to expect."

After a few minutes, Mrs. Sonia cradled the cards in her hand and pulled out the first card. Trying to piece together the meaning of the card, Lisa knew it wasn't a card that symbolized fortuity. She could tell by the illustration on the card that it was something bad.

Dire News

Mrs. Sonia pulled out the death card, and proceeded to inform Lisa that someone in her family was very ill and was going to die. The news struck a chord with Lisa because her sister was diagnosed with leukemia and was undergoing chemotherapy treatments; moreover, her 17-year-old cousin had died recently.

"I was like, 'Omigod.' I was shocked," recalls Lisa. "She then told me that I had a lot of darkness in my life caused by a curse."

Gauging the concern rising in Lisa, Mrs. Sonia knew that she had found an opening into Lisa. Mrs. Sonia told Lisa if she returned for more readings and healings, she could help her sister.

"She said I could assure the health of my sister if I came back consistently to see her," Lisa says. "I was at a very vulnerable state at the time, and once she brought in my sister, she got me. All I wanted was for my sister to get better."

In the meantime, Lisa was instructed to buy candles and rosary beads from Mrs. Sonia, purportedly from Jerusalem and Rome, and holy water so Mrs. Sonia could perform spiritual work in healing her sister and expunging the curse in her family.

The following week, Lisa returned to Mrs. Sonia. This time, she told Lisa that the curse was even worse than she had thought and more work needed to be done. More work translated to more money; Mrs. Sonia saw dollar signs in her future, rather than a foreboding curse in Lisa's.

At the end of this session, Mrs. Sonia ordered Lisa to bring in an egg for their next meeting. Confused and somewhat dubious, Lisa agreed to it. She figured she had invested hundreds of dollars on "healing items" already, and she wanted to see where Mrs. Sonia would take her next.

A Bloody Egg

"She cracked open the egg I brought from home and blood just came gushing out," says Lisa. "I was frightened. It was disgusting and scary and the image stayed with me for years. This was how she proved my curse."

At the time, Lisa did not know that Mrs. Sonia had used a sleight-of-hand trick and switched a prepared, bloody egg with the egg Lisa had brought from home.

Lisa said it was a very effective illusion. Before the bloody egg, she wasn't really frightened by Mrs. Sonia, but seeing crimson, viscous blood oozing out of the egg rattled her.

"She started bringing in these scary, religious undertones and after a short time, I was scared to death," Lisa says. "First it was the bloody egg and then it was the snake-in-the-jar-of-water trick. Somehow, using magic tricks, she got a snake into a jar of water right before my eyes. I believed her at the time."

As her meetings with Mrs. Sonia progressed, Lisa grew more scared and isolated. She felt that she couldn't tell anyone because Mrs. Sonia told her in order for the healing to work, she wasn't allowed to speak to anyone about their encounters. Lisa also felt embarrassed and ashamed.

"Here I am, a college-educated, working professional getting duped by a fortuneteller?" says Lisa. "Yes, it was embarrassing and I didn't know how to tell people."

Mrs. Sonia then told Lisa that the source of her curse came from her money, and it was tainted. She insisted that Lisa's money be cleansed by burning it or burying it in a graveyard.

Draining Lisa's Life Savings

Preying on her vulnerabilities, Mrs. Sonia told Lisa that she needed to transfer all the money in her bank account over to her. At this point, Lisa avoided and ignored Mrs. Sonia. But constant phone calls to her work and home together with reminders about the bloody egg stirred Lisa's already frayed emotions. Lisa says she opened up another bank account, deposited a small sum of money in it and turned it over to Mrs. Sonia, in hopes of repelling the psychic.

"But she knew that I had more money in another account, and she got upset with me," says Lisa. "I hesitated in giving her my bank account information because my life savings were in there."

The badgering for Lisa's money continued, and she was constantly reminded of her curse and the imminent death of her sister.

In retrospect Lisa says, "She just wanted more money from me and I had nowhere else to turn. I had recurring visions and images of the bloody eggs and I just wanted her to leave me alone. So I gave her all the money in my bank account, which was $15,000."

After amassing a large amount of money from Lisa, Mrs. Sonia never contacted Lisa again. But that didn't mean that Lisa didn't live in fear every day.

"I didn't tell anyone for 10 years," she says. "I was afraid if I reported this, first no one would care and second, she would come after me and my family. I just wanted to forget about her. It was very difficult though, because I'd lost my life savings, everything."

Fighting Back

Living in silence and shame, it wasn't until she saw a program on television in July 1999 that Lisa realized that she had been a victim of fraud and extortion. *Dateline NBC* featured a sting operation by New York police on fortunetellers.

The program also showed the egg trick that was carried out on Lisa, and uncovered how the psychics in New York City encouraged customers to buy candles, rosary beads and prayer cards. "I sat there, watching the show, thinking, 'the same thing happened to me,'" Lisa says. "I was relieved, but saddened that this was happening to other people all over the country."

She did some research and found out that sting operations in other cities like Boston, Baton Rouge and Los Angeles had busted psychics who swindled hundreds of thousands of dollars out of unsuspecting victims. But it was 2002 before Lisa finally called the SFPD and told her story. A December 2002 newspaper article about a proposed ordinance to regulate the city's fortunetellers after several victims lost upwards of $200,000, prompted Lisa to talk.

"It took something like this to come forward. I couldn't keep silent any longer because I wanted people to know about this," Lisa says. "The fear tactics these psychics use are so powerful that it keeps you from talking."

Lisa's case landed on the desk of Inspector Greg Ovanessian, who has worked in the fraud detail unit at the SFPD for 13 years. Ovanessian heard Lisa's story and started an investigation into Mrs. Sonia. "This is the only complaint against Mrs. Sonia, but this psychic left San Francisco long ago," says Ovanessian. "However, our victim was able to articulate clearly her experience and she kept all the evidence associated with the psychic."

All of these are key elements in prosecuting Mrs. Sonia, he said, but it is up to the District Attorney's Office to decide whether or not the evidence and statements are enough to substantiate a prosecution. He added that if prosecutors decline to take the case, then unfortunately, it's the end of the road for Lisa's case. In order for psychics or fortune tellers to be prosecuted for criminal activities, there needs to have been false representation.

"If I'm sitting across from you and I tell you that you'll have great things coming your way, then that's okay," says Ovanessian. "But when I tell you that you need to give me money, to buy candles or this will happen, but it never does, or that you will die, then there's fraud and a crime here."

This investigation is working against time. There is a statute of limitations of four years from the time the victim discovered that he or she was a victim of fraud, according to Ovanessian. "The television program Lisa saw was aired in July of 1999, and we're coming up on July 2003," he said. "The clock is ticking, and we're hoping to issue a warrant for Mrs. Sonia, or whatever her real name is, by July."

Scams A-plenty

Since 1990, Ovanessian has received 53 reports on fortune-teller frauds from all areas of the city. There are currently 70 psychic shops in San Francisco, not including astrology readers. Ovanessian says he has not received any complaints about those 70 or the astrology readers, but adds that there may be more fortunetellers who operate from their homes or in rented rooms in stores.

He said Asian Pacific Americans [APAs], particularly women, are prime targets for fortuneteller scams and make easy victims. "It doesn't take a lot of convincing on the part of the psychic to persuade them about the concept of good and bad spirits, or the fact that there are evil forces lingering," said Ovanessian. "Also, APAs tend to keep large amounts of cash at home. And language isn't a barrier. Many of the APAs who go to fortunetellers are highly educated or are born here."

Laurel Pallock, an investigator for the Consumer Mediation Program of the District Attorney's Office, said that after receiving numerous complaints about fortuneteller scams, it was obvious that the city needed a better mechanism to regulate the psychics. "I decided to see if we could regulate this industry, as in others like taxi drivers and masseuses," she says.

"This would require fortunetellers to get a permit. They would get their backgrounds checked, have their photos taken and get fingerprinted."

This way, Pallock said, the city would have some kind of record. If a complaint were made, the police would have a name and an address with which to work. Currently, psychics are not required to hold permits. "I proposed this legislation to the supervisor's office [in 2002], and presently it's still being drafted and we're waiting on getting a hearing date," she says. "We should have the final draft by next month, but with the city's budget and the war [in Iraq], this wasn't that important in the scheme of things."

Stopping Exploitation

In December 2002, District Attorney Terence Hallinan and Supervisor Aaron Peskin held a joint conference announcing the proposed ordinance. At the conference, a Chinese American woman spoke about how she was conned out of $17,000 by her psychic. There was another Japanese American woman who was told by her psychic that if she didn't turn over money, her young daughter would bleed to death.

"I was a little reluctant to move it forward in the beginning," Peskin says. "But Laurel did a good job in telling me the stories about the fraud victims and how they were targeted at vulnerable stages in their lives."

Peskin said he was wary of getting involved with this legislation because it might have been seen as discriminatory toward gypsies. But he said this issue affects every community and every ethnicity. "I have absolutely no problem with the age-old craft of fortunetelling," Peskin says. "But we need to regulate this business so that we protect where there's exploitation of people. We want to create an ordinance to let consumers have public oversight. This isn't a way for the city to make money."

Ovanessian said many who go to fortunetellers are fun-seekers looking for entertainment, but also there are those who may have emotional or relationship problems who haven't been able to get answers by any other means.

Lisa said she still has lasting psychological effects from her painful experience, and it has left a lasting impression on her. She still gets anxious when she sees psychic stores or ads, or when she writes a check or withdraws money from the bank.

But for now, Lisa is trying to move on with her life. She's relieved to see that the wheels are in motion for the criminal investigation and the proposed city ordinance. "What started out as a $20 love reading ended up costing me $15,000," Lisa says. "And she didn't even tell me about my love life."

Psychic Hotlines Are Just Out to Get Money

Dougall Fraser

Psychic hotlines are a multimillion-dollar business. Thousands of people call these lines and pay by the minute to hear their fortune, ask supposed psychics about their problems, and get advice about the future. Dougall Fraser is a psychic who worked on a psychic hotline for several months. Fraser considers himself to be a genuine psychic who can divine information about people and help them make their way in life. As a budding professional in the psychic business, he thought that working for a psychic hotline would be an ideal job. He would be able to use his unusual talent to help many people, and he would earn substantial money doing it.

As Fraser describes in this selection, however, not long after he started working for a psychic hotline he began to be disillusioned. He writes that his employer pressured him to keep callers on the line for a long time to run up their bill, and he discovered that the company was sending out letters, supposedly from him, telling people that he urgently needed to speak to them—another ploy for separating people from their money. Fraser finally decided that all psychic hotlines were simply out to gain money, not to help people. He left the world of telephone psychics thoroughly disillusioned.

Fraser is a professional psychic in New York. This selection is excerpted from his memoir, But You Knew That Already, *which details his childhood and young adulthood as he comes to grips with his psychic abilities, career aspirations, and relationships.*

Dougall Fraser, *But You Knew That Already: What a Psychic Can Teach You About Life.* Emmaus, PA: Rodale, 2005, pp. 106–15. Copyright © 2005 by Dougall Fraser. Reproduced by permission.

I read at a psychic fair at a women's university while religious protestors waved signs out front. I read at bookstores and coffeehouses. Everything that a struggling 20-year-old psychic could do, I did it. This was around the time—late 1990s—that psychic phone lines were tremendously popular.

You couldn't turn on the TV without seeing an ad. They had always intrigued me; I thought it seemed like the ideal job for a psychic. I believed every word of the infomercials. It was my dream to work on a psychic hotline. It seemed too good to be true—I could work from home and do what I loved. I was hearing at the psychic fairs that some people were making $2,000 or $3,000 a month working psychic lines, plus bonuses. That was big money to me.

I called the Kenny Kingston Psychic Hotline and got hired on the spot over the phone. I didn't realize [it] before, but it seemed like if you could talk, you were hired. They couldn't have cared less if you were psychic. I was in. I was asked to get a second phone line installed in my house and was sent a packet of information in the mail.

Number 1,499

The way it worked was that I dialed in to an 800 number and heard a broadcast message. A woman would come on and say something like, "Hey, everybody, commercials are on at 11 tonight. We're going to have very strong hits between midnight and 3 A.M. " All the psychics were arranged on a priority list, so when I started, out of 1,500 psychics who worked there, I was number 1,499. When someone wanted to call in for a reading, they were plugged in to psychic number 1. The second caller went to psychic number 2, and so on down the line. There would have to be 1,499 simultaneous calls for me to get one.

But I didn't realize that on my first night. The first time I logged in to the system, alerting them that I was plugged in and ready to receive calls, I was so excited! Of course, I was trying to be very spiritual. I had soft music on and candles lighted, and I was sitting with my tarot cards in front of me, ready for fire. Twenty minutes later, I kind of leaned back and relaxed a bit. An hour into it, I picked up a book. By 2 A.M. I had the radio on and was dancing around the room, wearing my headset. Finally, the phone rang at 4 A.M. I leaped on it. Protocol was to ask callers for their name and date of birth.

"Kenny Kingston Psychic Hotline. My name is Dougall. May I please have your name and date of birth?" I said breathlessly, all in a rush.

The young man on the other end happened to be 18 on that very day (you had to be 18 years old to call a 900 number). It was ridiculous; I'm sure he was probably 13. He said, "All I want to know is when I'm going to lose my virginity."

I said, "You've got to be kidding me."

And he hung up. That was it. My first call. My only call, as it turned out, for the entire week. I was logged in to the system for 20 hours—from 11 P.M. until 3 A.M. five nights in a row—and received that one phone call. When I had signed up to work on the Kenny Kingston Psychic Hotline, I'd been promised that I would make between $12 and $24 an hour because I'd be paid by the talking minute. But if the phone didn't ring, I got nothing.

Madly Ringing Phone

I called the office the day I got my check in the mail for my first week of work. My net pay was about $1.50. I complained, "I was online for 20 hours and only got one phone call."

The supervisor was very nice. She explained the whole priority process to me and said, "Well, I'll increase your priority and we'll see what happens." She bumped me up in the system to probably number 25 or so. That night I logged in, and the phone didn't stop ringing. As soon as I put the receiver down, a new call started ringing in. I did 10 readings an hour, from midnight until 4 in the morning. I literally could not get off the phone. I couldn't pee; I couldn't stand up—that phone rang every 7 seconds. . . .

When I logged out at 4 A.M. that first night after being bumped up, I was freaked-out. I could not even do it the next night—it was too weird and scary. The Kenny Kingston Psychic Hotline was not doing it for me. So I quit working for them and turned to a classier venue, the Psychic Friends Network. I had heard through some fellow seers that it was much better. I called the main office in Atlanta and spoke to someone in personnel.

A Better Network

The woman on the other end of the phone explained the whole Psychic Friends Network to me. I had to send in letters of recommendation, a picture, and a résumé. They required proof that whoever worked for them had been a practicing psychic for 10 years. This was a tough one for me; I was only 20 years old. So in my application I just left off my date of birth. I wrote a letter saying I had studied tarot, taught meditation and Reiki, and been a practicing psychic for 10 years. I got a call back from what I called ESP Central, and they set up three test readings. They were carefully screening me, and I was glad. My only worry was that I wouldn't meet their standards.

I dialed a number in Colorado for my first test reading.

"Hi, this is Alan. Is this Dougall?"

"Yes, sir. I'm a little nervous."

"Don't be."

"Alan, the first thing I see around you is blue. Did a relationship just end that involved the other party cheating?"

We were on the phone for about 10 minutes. He seemed genuinely impressed that I was able to target the demise of his marriage after he discovered his wife's affair. I was also able to come up with his current girlfriend's name and that he really didn't want to marry her. He was blown away. Then he went through his list of questions.

"What if someone called you and wanted to get their boyfriend back? Would you teach them how to put a spell on him?"

"Absolutely not," I said. "There is nothing anyone can do to help you get someone back if they don't want to be with you. You need to pray for the highest good for everyone concerned and make your peace with the situation." That was the right answer—he had to make sure I wouldn't manipulate the callers.

"What if someone asks for your home number and wants to talk to you privately for less money?"

That sounded just fine to me, but I knew that operators monitored the calls, so I said, "I would never do that! I'm here to make money for the Psychic Friends Network!" I was the perfect applicant. . . .

There is a constant, 24-hour-a-day stream of calls coming in to the Psychic Friends Network. But I learned that if I logged in during the middle of the day, when commercials weren't constantly running—let's say at 2 in the afternoon—I got only three or four calls an hour. I liked that pace. I hadn't liked working in the middle of the night, lonely souls pouring out their hearts at 4 A.M.; having breakfast at 2 P.M. This was more like regular working hours.

The people who called Psychic Friends Network were a more sophisticated bunch, though there were still a few who called and wanted to speak to [Psychic Friends spokesperson, singer] Dionne Warwick. I'd be like, "Lady, I'm at home in my pajamas, and I've never met Dionne Warwick." No, I didn't really say that, but I wanted to. I used to turn on the TV across the room and monitor the commercials closely while I was logged in, to see at what point people started dialing in. Was it Dionne's tear that moved them? Was it when [actress] Vicki Lawrence was so wowed by her reading? The whole marketing process fascinated me. And even though I understood the business behind the whole entertainment aspect of the info-mercial, a big part of me still wanted to believe in it.

An Uneasy Feeling

The Psychic Friends Network certainly felt like the most repu-table of all the psychic phone lines. With every paycheck, I re-ceived a whole sales sheet breaking out each of my calls, show-ing how long each person had stayed on the line, how many people had specifically requested me—everything. It was highly professional and organized on one hand, but I was starting to get pushed in a direction that made me uneasy. I was urged to sign my callers up for a special "club," so at the end of each call, I had to ask, "Would you like to join our Psy-chic Circle? For $9.95 a month, you'll get a voice mail system that gives you a free astrological reading every day!" I think what the company really wanted was a name and an address with a matching credit card number that could be automati-cally charged $9.95 every month.

I started getting bombarded with training brochures from the corporate office in the mail. It was never as flat-out as "How to Keep Callers on the Phone." They had cheery titles like "Ideas to Make Your Readings Better!" For example, start readings by asking your clients to count backward from 10 to 1 and center their thoughts. Well, that's an additional 10 sec-onds of time charged. I really wanted to believe that it was a good company and I was doing good work, but it was getting harder.

Let's say you as a caller decided to call the Psychic Friends Network. You would dial their 900 number and speak to a psychic who worked there. But say 2 hours later you're watch-ing a commercial for the Nell Carter Psychic Hotline and de-cide to call there, too, maybe get a second opinion. You would dial a different 900 number and speak to someone else. But on my end, whichever number you dialed, my phone would ring. Whenever I lifted my handset, the first thing I'd hear was a whispered, "Nell, Nell." (Or "Psychic Friends," or "Kenny.") In the beginning, I didn't know what the little whisper meant, so I ignored it and said, "Psychic Friends Network. This is Sean [the pseudonym Fraser used while working for this hotline]. May I help you?"

The person on the other end of the phone was sometimes surprised. "Wait a minute. I just called the Nell Carter hotline."

All the Same Company

"That's impossible. I work at the Psychic Friends Network." This happened a few times until I finally figured out what was going on. They were all the same company. If you called Love-Lines, you got me. You called the Linda Georgian Psychic Hotline, you got me. You called Psychic Friends, you got me. All the smaller companies were merely divisions of the same big corporation.

From my impression, there seemed to be three huge corporations that owned three or more lines each. And the psychics who worked for one of these companies worked for them all. I quickly learned to catch that little whisper in my ear at the beginning of each call. It was to alert me to which number the caller dialed so I would answer the phone correctly. "Thank you for calling the Zodiac Hotline. . . ." "Thank you for calling Astrology Readings. . . ." All me.

I became further disillusioned but still wanted to believe I had a great job at a good company. But it was getting harder. I had a regular caller, Champagne, on the Psychic Friends Network. She called in every day at 11 o'clock and always requested me. She had the same two questions for me every day: "When is my husband getting out of jail?" and "When am I getting my welfare check?" One day, I couldn't take it anymore. I said, "Champagne, the next time you want to call me, I want you to take $50, open a window, and throw it out. Because that's what you're doing every day. It is a complete waste of your money." She hung up on me in a huff, and that was the end of Champagne.

Every now and again, I'd get the frisky callers. I'd be saying, "As I'm turning over the cards, I see . . ." and they'd be interrupting every 5 seconds: "What are you wearing?"

An Urgent Letter

Most of the callers really started to depress me. The last straw was when I started getting calls from people saying, "Sean, I got your letter saying you really needed to speak with me urgently . . ." and I'd say, "What are you talking about? I didn't send you any letter." They'd insist, "I have your letter right here. You're Sean at extension 5842, right?" I didn't worry about it too much until one day when I got a call from a woman who was livid.

"You sent my husband a letter, Sean. You said that you have important things to tell him about love and life and money." She paused, then really screamed, "My husband's dead! He just died of cancer! He was desperate. That's the only reason he would have called you! You don't have any f--king thing to tell him about love or life!" She really went off on me. I couldn't figure what all this letter stuff was about, so I called the line myself and posed as a caller. And 10 days later, I got a postcard in my mailbox, saying, "Dear Dougall, Your psychic Tom at extension 4821 needs to talk to you immediately about urgent matters concerning . . ."

I felt like a hooker. The ploy disgusted me. To this day, I believe that working one of those lines is one small step above being a prostitute. Those letters sent in my name were the end of it for me. Several years later, when I had achieved some success in the psychic world, I was offered my own psychic hotline. I turned it down flat. More than once, I have been offered a lot of money to lend my name to one. There is not enough money in the world for me to do something like that. Ever.

No Good One

Those corporations were making millions and millions of dollars. They had more than 1,000 psychics working for them. The psychics were paid 15 cents for every minute they were on the phone, while callers were being charged $3.95 a minute. The biggest check I had ever gotten was for $195. My whole experiment with psychic hotlines lasted about 6 months, and over those 6 months, I tried working for them all. For a long time, I just couldn't let it go—the idea of doing my work, being psychic and helping people, from home, and the lure of good money. I kept thinking that I just had to find the right line and it would be the perfect job, but there was no good one.

Fortune-Tellers Fool Their Victims with Clever Tactics

The Straight Dope Science Advisory Board

Various experts have studied psychics for many years and have found explanations for why they can seem so successful in telling people's fortunes. According to the Straight Dope Science Advisory Board, successful psychics use a variety of clever tactics to make their clients think they are seeing the past or foreseeing the future. In this selection, the Straight Dope authors describe some of the tricks fortune-tellers use. For example, they may make statements that sound specific but actually could apply to the lives of many people. Fortune-tellers may also cleverly phrase statements so that whether their guesses are right or wrong, they appear to be right. The authors advise people to maintain skepticism about fortune-tellers and not waste money on readings.

The Straight Dope is a popular syndicated question-and-answer column first appearing in the Chicago Reader *newspaper in 1973. The column answers readers' questions on every conceivable topic. Articles from the newspaper column are reprinted on The Straight Dope Web site, www.straightdope.com, which also includes a readers' forum and other features.*

What's impressive about psychics is the number of times people go to a reading, or watch one of those "hotline to heaven" shows, and say, "He told us things he couldn't possibly have known." Psychics and their fans say it's evidence of genuine psychic ability. But keep a couple things in mind:

(1) To date there's no scientific proof of the existence of "real" psychics. A stage or TV performance or a personal reading doesn't prove anything. Yes, a psychic can come up with amazingly accurate "hits." But people who are NOT psychics

The Straight Dope Science Advisory Board, "How Come TV Psychics Seem So Convincing?" www.straightdope.com, 2003. Reproduced by permission.

and make no pretense of having psychic powers can do readings and get equally good results.

As an example, Ian Rowland (whom we consulted for this report) is an entertainer who claims no psychic ability. He has given TV demonstrations posing as a tarot reader, an astrologer, a clairvoyant, and a spirit medium (someone who talks to the dead.) He scored just as many hits as the "genuine" psychics even though he openly admits he isn't psychic. He got his impressive results using a technique called cold reading. More on this later.

No Scientific Evidence

(2) Demonstrations of psychic ability aren't considered evidence unless they're done under scientifically-controlled conditions—which is a fancy way of saying no fudging, trickery, or cheating is permitted. Psychic readings done in someone's living room, a carnival booth, or a TV studio aren't scientifically controlled. The search for evidence of psychic powers has been going on around the world for over a century—the American Society for Psychical Research was founded in 1885. All that research and effort has failed to produce a single psychic who can demonstrate genuine psychic ability.

So how do entertainers, carnival fortune tellers, tarot readers, and others get those amazing results? Let's correct a few overly facile explanations.

- It has nothing to do with the gullibility or stupidity of the subject (the person being read). Even intelligent, perceptive people can be taken in if they don't know how cold readings work, just as they can be fooled by a stage magician's sleight of hand. Psychics do rely on the subject's co-operation, often unwitting.

- Some people dismiss readings as nothing but vague generalizations. Sure, psychics can be vague at times. But often they give very specific information—or at least they seem to.

- You may have heard that stage psychics read body language and make shrewd, Sherlock Holmes-style deductions about the person being read. Again, that's only a small part of the story. Most deductions are fairly obvious, like noticing a wedding ring or lack thereof.

So how do stage psychics do it? They rely on three main techniques:

(a) Hot readings, where the psychic has secretly obtained advance information about the person being read.

(b) Cold readings, where the psychic has no advance information, but instead shrewdly elicits facts during the reading and plays them back to the subject, to the latter's amazement. This is the most common technique used by entertainers, and we'll spend the most time on it.

(c) TV editing.

OK, let's dig in.

Hot Readings

In a hot reading, the psychic has surreptitiously gained information about the subject in advance. There are many ways of doing this, ranging from simple eavesdropping to sophisticated espionage techniques.

The spokespeople for the TV psychics strongly deny using such techniques. *Skeptical Inquirer* magazine sent people to one well-known TV psychic's show and had them talk about phony deceased relatives while waiting in line. If the psychic had mentioned any of those names or people, it would have been clear evidence of secret intelligence gathering—but he didn't. So we have no evidence that TV psychics use hot reading techniques, and I suspect for most it's a minor part of their arsenal.

Cold Readings

Sophisticated intelligence gathering is seldom necessary. Cold reading, the technique used by entertainers who claim no psychic powers, can explain most performances.

Cold reading is a kind of interactive psychological game, where you fish for information and give the impression of knowing more than you do. The term "cold" means that the psychic has no advance knowledge.

In this report, we can only cover the basics of cold reading. With the author's permission, we've taken most of our information from Ian Rowland's book, listed below in the resources section.

The Set-Up. The psychic usually sets up his readings so that everyone has to play by his rules. For example, the psychic announces that he can't always be precise, and he invites the client (the person to whom he is giving the reading) to help him "interpret" what comes up. That sounds plausible, but it's just a way of saying, "I'm going to leave plenty of room for interpretation, to increase my chances of getting a hit."

Often the psychic encourages the subject to have a positive, cooperative attitude, and suggests this will help the success of the reading. The goal is to stop people from asking awkward questions or being too analytical about what's going on. The psychic is also subtly encouraging the client to offer information during the course of the reading, and many people do so, often without realizing it.

Rapid patter and an expressive verbal style, a la Professor Harold Hill in *The Music Man*, are also helpful.

Elements of the Reading

Okay, so with the subject warmed up and conditioned to play by the psychic's rules, what next? The psychic pretends to give one or two bits of potentially significant information. In reality, he doesn't have any information; he's just taking a few stabs and hoping to get lucky.

For example, he might say, "I'm seeing the end of August, maybe the twenty-sixth of August or a date close to that, which I think is significant for you, and a man—let me think—a man related to you, who wears glasses." That sounds very specific, but think how much scope such a statement leaves for interpretation! Almost any date from August 20 to August 31 will do. It could be a birthday, death date, anniversary, vacation, social function, or important decision. It could be significant personally, socially, or professionally, every year or just one particular year. The man could be a husband, partner, brother, relative, friend, colleague, doctor or plumber (the word "related to" is pretty ambiguous, isn't it?). He could be alive or dead, well-known or a distant acquaintance. In short, there are countless ways that the subject might interpret this comment as a hit.

The psychic knows some psychology: People will remember the bits that seem to connect, and forget those that don't. For example, the subject may respond tentatively: "Well, my father's birthday was early August, and he wore glasses ..." The psychic will focus there and the subject will remember it as a hit, even though "late August" was wrong.

That's just one example. Rowland describes 38 different ways to offer initial statements that seem meaningful, but in fact are just guesses. The initial statements can be related to character or personality, or can pertain to facts and events. Here are a few more examples, using Rowland's terminology.

- "Barnum statements" sound specific but really apply to most people, most of the time. For example: "Though you might not always admit it, you have a deep-rooted need for other people's approval, especially when you know you have done something well. You tend to be a bit more honest than many people you meet." Does this sound like you? You probably think it's pretty close. Most people would say the same.

- "Rainbow" statements describe personality traits so as to cover all the bases, like this: "You have a very generous and giving nature, and can be very unselfish, although if you're honest about it, there have been times when you've acted in perhaps quite a selfish way."

- "Trivia statistics" are statements that are actually more likely to hit than they at first appear. The psychic might say, "I've got the spirit of an elderly lady here, and she's mentioning a box full of old photographs or souvenirs." That sounds specific, but in fact most people have something like this in their homes.

- "Fuzzy statements" like the "late August" example already given may sound specific but in fact are wild-ass guesses with plenty of room for interpretation.

These techniques work well during a one-on-one reading but are even more effective before an audience in a theater or TV studio. The psychic might say, "I'm seeing an elderly man, some sort of uniform, possibly military." Even with a small audience, it would be rare if no one could find a connection to "some sort of uniform."

Clever Tactics

Cold reading isn't just clever guesswork. Psychics can look like they're giving information when in fact they're subtly fishing for it. For example, the psychic says, "I see a car, a blue car," and then prompts for feedback by saying, "now why would that be?" or "is this making sense to you?" It sounds as if the psychic is giving information, but in reality he's trying to extract it. Again, most people could find some connection with a "blue car" at some point in their lives.

Another clever tactic is what Rowland calls the "vanishing negative." For example, the psychic says, "You don't work with children, do you?" The question has been expressed as a negative, so if the subject replies, "Yes, I do," the psychic says, "Yes, I thought so." If the subject replies, "No, I don't," the psychic says, "Yes, I thought not." It's a hit either way!

In normal conversation, a flat statement can be seen as right or wrong. But in cold readings, the psychic can twist things so that he's always right. Or, at worst, he can find an escape hatch.

Suppose the psychic says, "You have a connection with the name Charles or Charlie?" The subject himself may be called Charles, or know someone by that name. If not, the psychic encourages the subject to think harder. Any connection will do—social or professional, friend or relative, near or far, past or present so it's very likely that the subject will think of a Charles eventually. Or perhaps a sound-alike name like Charlene or Chad. But if not, the psychic can just say, "Well, watch out for that name. Because I think it's going to be significant in the near future." And the psychic has gotten neatly off the hook.

Another example of an escape hatch: The psychic can claim he's right, but the subject doesn't know it! This ruse is often used by so-called "pet psychics." How can the client possibly know what the dog is really thinking?

Using such techniques, the skilled cold-reader can get impressive results. Rowland, for instance, did a cold reading on TV that was deemed "99.5% accurate"—full details are in his book.

TV Editing

Cold readings work just fine in live settings. But when the psychic is performing on TV, a whole new realm of manipulation is available. The show you see on your TV is the result of a long process of taping and editing. The production team's task isn't to present a sober scientific account but to produce an entertaining show. Wrong guesses and blind alleys are boring and can be skillfully edited out. Readings that don't go well can disappear in the editing room. Uncooperative people don't appear on the aired program.

In the *Skeptical Inquirer* article, James Underdown cites some examples. He smuggled a tape recorder into live sessions by a couple of stage psychics and compared the edited versions with the reality. Reality lost.

Underdown says, "Virtually everything you see on TV has been precisely edited for both time and content. . . . The aired tape does not represent how the readings went in the studio. The aired versions show a much more successful account of the reading."

The power of editing is enormous. If the psychic makes twenty guesses and gets three hits, we wouldn't be very impressed. But edit out the 17 wrong guesses and show only the three correct ones, and the viewing audience's estimation of the psychic's ability is likely to rise substantially.

Comments can be edited out of sequence, so that a response to an innocuous statement can appear to be a positive response to a wild guess.

Most people are fairly savvy about "movie magic" but fail to realize that similar editing techniques can be (and are) applied to TV shows. It's made to feel live, but it's not.

In sum, the readings of TV psychics don't look so impressive once you understand the techniques involved. That doesn't mean you can't enjoy the performance, just as you can enjoy a good magician's sleight-of-hand. But you'd do well to maintain your skepticism—and keep one hand on your wallet.

Resources

We want to give full credit to Ian Rowland's book, *The Full Facts Book of Cold Reading* (3rd edition, 2002, published in the UK). The book provides, in about 240 pages, "a comprehensive guide to the most persuasive psychological manipulation technique in the world and its application to psychic readings."

See *Skeptical Inquirer*, vol. 27, no. 5 (September–October 2003), pp. 41–44, for a brilliant article by James Underdown, looking specifically at TV psychics John Edward and James Van Praagh.

Palm Reading Is Bunk

Michael Shermer

Michael Shermer is a science writer, founder of the Skeptics Society, and editor of Skeptic, *a journal published by the society. Shermer and the Skeptics Society promote rational thinking and are skeptical of the claims people make about practices such as fortune-telling, which cannot be proven scientifically. In the following selection, Shermer describes his experience posing as a "psychic" on a television program. The program was part of a Public Television Network series focusing on questions of interest to scientists and laypeople alike.*

Shermer determined that he would tell the fortunes of five people, using a different fortune-telling method with each. Shermer was convinced that with no experience whatsoever, and with no belief in psychic abilities, he could nonetheless successfully make people think he was able to foretell their future. This excerpt focuses on his session as a palm reader. Shermer describes his success at this practice and concludes that because he could fool customers with relative ease, so could any charlatan. Shermer considers fortune-tellers to be frauds who take advantage of vulnerable people.

Shermer has published several books, including Why People Believe Weird Things: Pseudoscience, Superstition, and Other Confusions of Our Time; How We Believe: Science, Skepticism, and the Search for God; Science Friction: Where the Known Meets the Unknown; *and* The Skeptic Encyclopedia of Pseudoscience.

On Wednesday, January 15, 2003, I filmed a television show with Bill Nye in Seattle, Washington, for a new PBS science series entitled *Eyes of Nye*. This series is an adult-

Michael Shermer, "Psychic for a Day," *Skeptic*, vol. 10, no. 1, 2003, pp. 1–6. Reproduced by permission.

oriented version of Bill's wildly successful 100-episode children's series *Bill Nye the Science Guy*. This 30-minute segment focused on psychics and talking to the dead. Although I have analyzed the process and written about it extensively in *Skeptic, Scientific American, How We Believe*, and on www.skep tic.com, I have had little experience actually doing psychic readings. Bill and I thought it would be a good test of the effectiveness of the technique and the receptivity of people to it to see if an inexperienced person could do it armed with just a little knowledge.

Although the day of the taping was set weeks in advance, I did absolutely nothing to prepare until the day before. This made me especially nervous because psychic readings are a form of improvisational acting, which takes both talent and practice. And I made matters even harder on myself by convincing Bill and the producers that if we were going to do this we should use a number of different psychic techniques, including Tarot cards, palm reading, astrology, and psychic mediumship, under the theory that these are all "props" used to stage a psychodrama called cold reading (reading someone "cold" without any prior knowledge). I am now more convinced than ever that cheating (getting information ahead of time on subjects) is not a necessary part of a successful reading.

The Setting

I read five different people, all women that the production staff had selected and about whom I was told absolutely nothing other than the date and time of their birth (in order to prepare an astrological chart). I had no contact with any of the subjects until they sat down in front of me for the taping. There was no conversation between us until the cameras started rolling. The setting was a sound stage at KCTS, the PBS member station in Seattle. Since sound stages can have a rather cold feel to them, and because the environment in which a reading is done is a key factor in generating a receptive mindset, I instructed the production staff to set up two comfortable chairs with a small table between them, with a lace cloth covering the table and candles on and around the table, all sitting on a beautiful Persian rug. Soft, colored lighting and incense increased the "spiritual" ambiance. . . .

The Palm Reading

My second reading was on a female college student, age 19. Palm reading is the best of the psychic props because, as in the Tarot cards, there is something specific to refer to, but it has the added advantage of allowing the reader to make physical contact with the subject. I could not remember what all the lines on a palm are supposed to represent, so while I was memorizing the Tarot cards my daughter Devin did a google .com image search for me and downloaded a palm chart.

I mainly focused on the Life, Head, Heart, and Health lines, and for added effect threw in some blather about the Marriage, Money, and Fate lines. Useful nonsense includes:

—If the Head and Life lines are connected it means that there was an early dependence on family.

—If Head and Life lines are not connected it means the client has declared independence early.

—The degree of separation between the Head and Heart lines indicates the degree of dependence or independence between the head and the heart for making decisions.

—The strength of the Head line indicates the thinking style—intuitive or rational.

—Breaks in the Head line may mean there was a head injury, or that the subject gets headaches or something happened to the head at some time in the subject's life.

Thumb Angles

On one web page I downloaded some material about the angles of the thumbs in relation to to the hands that was quite useful. You have the subject place both hands palm down on the table, and then observe whether they are relaxed or tight and whether the fingers are close together or spread apart. This purportedly indicates how uptight or relaxed someone is, how extroverted or introverted they are, how confident or insecure they feel, etc. According to one palm reader a small thumb angle "reveals that you are a person who does not rush into doing things. You are cautious and wisely observe the situation before taking action. You are not pushy about getting your way." A medium thumb angle "reveals that you do things both for yourself and for others willingly. You are not overly mental about what you are going to do, so you don't waste a lot of time doing unnecessary planning for each job." And a big thumb angle "reveals that you are eager to jump in and get things done right away. You do things quickly, confidently, and pleasurably because you like to take charge and get the job done." Conveniently, you can successfully use any of these descriptions with anyone.

It turns out that you can tell the handedness of a person because the dominant hand is a little larger and more muscular. That gave me an opening to tell Subject #2, who was left-handed, that she was right-brain dominant, which means that she puts more emphasis on intuition than on intellect, that she is herself very intuitive ([in his book *The Full Facts Book of Cold Reading* Ian] Rowland says that a great ruse is to flatter the subjects with praise about their own psychic powers), and that her wisdom comes more from real world experience than traditional book learning. She nodded furiously in agreement.

According to the various palm reading "experts," you are supposed to comment on the color and texture of the skin, hair on the back of the hand, and general shape of the hands. Any major discrepancy between the two hands is supposed to be a sign of areas where subjects have departed from their inherited potential. The psychic should also take note of the shape of the fingers. The outer phalanges of the fingers (the finger tips) represent spiritual or idealistic aspects of the person, the middle phalanges everyday and practical aspects, and the lower phalanges the emotional aspects of personality. I found it most effective to rub my fingers over the mounds of flesh on each finger segment while commenting on this subject's personality. . . .

High Probability Guesses

For this reading I threw in a few [of Rowland's suggested] high probability guesses, starting with [stating that I "see"] a white car. It turns out that her 99-year old grandmother had a white car, which gave me an opening to comment about the special nature of her relationship with her grandmother, which was spot on. Then I tried the [generic statement that I sense something about an] out-of-date calendar, which did not draw an affirmative response from my mark, so I recovered by backing off toward a more general comment: "Well . . . what I'm getting here is something about a transition from one period in your life to another," which elicited a positive affirmation from the subject that she was thinking of switching majors. . . .

Wanton Depravity

I am not a psychic nor do I believe that ESP, telepathy, clairvoyance, clairaudience, or any of the other forms of psi power have any basis whatsoever in fact. There is not a shred of evidence that any of this is real, and the fact that I could do it reasonably well with only one day of preparation shows just how vulnerable people are to these very effective nostrums. I can only imagine what I could do with considerable experience. Give me six hours a day of practice for a couple of weeks and I have no doubt that I could easily host a successful syndicated television series and increase my current bank balance by several orders of magnitude. There—if not for the grace of evolved moral sentiments and guilt-laden scruples—go I. I cannot do this for one simple reason—it is wrong. I have lost both of my parents—my father suddenly of a heart attack in 1986, my mother slowly from brain cancer in 2000—and I cannot imagine anything more insulting to the dead, and more insidious to the living, than constructing a fantasy that they are hovering nearby in the psychic aether, awaiting some self-proclaimed psychic conduit to reveal to me breathtaking insights about scars on my knees, broken appliances and unfulfilled desires. This is worse than wrong. It is wanton depravity.

Epilogue: Analyzing the Evidence

As the introduction to this book indicates, fortune-tellers occupy a respected place in many world cultures. But in other cultures, fortune-telling is widely regarded as a superstitious holdover from more primitive times. These different beliefs are influenced by cultural traditions, religious and educational influences, and personal experience. Which view of fortune-telling is true? You can begin to shape your beliefs about this controversial topic by critically examining the evidence provided by fortune-tellers, by those who have studied fortune-telling scientifically, and by those who have had their fortunes told. Each article in this book provides various kinds of evidence and makes various kinds of arguments favoring or challenging the validity of fortune-telling. Some articles directly contradict others. It is your job to decide which articles present a truthful and reasonable case for—or against—fortune-telling.

You can do this by reading the articles critically. This does not mean that you criticize, or say negative things about, an article. It means that you analyze and evaluate what the author says. This chapter describes a critical-reading technique and allows you to practice it by evaluating the articles in this book.

The Author

In deciding whether an article is good support for or against fortune-telling, it can be helpful to learn more about the author. Consider whether the author has any special qualifications for writing about the subject. Has the author conducted—or read about—scientific research related to fortune-telling? Is the author a practicing fortune-teller? Some authors may have a vested interest in persuading you that fortune-telling is—or is not—a valid practice. For example, it is advantageous for people who earn their living by telling fortunes to persuade you that fortune-telling is valid. However, this does not mean that every fortune-teller will dishonestly try to persuade you. Part of your job as a critical reader is to decide whether the author presents the evidence fairly and accurately or if he or she unfairly stacks the deck in favor of one point of view.

As you read, think about the author's likely motives in writing the article. In this book, the editor has provided at least a small amount of information about each author. Use this information to start forming your opinion about the author's claims.

Hypothetical Reasoning

Whether or not you know anything about the author, you can evaluate an article on its own merits by using hypothetical reasoning. This is a method for determining whether something makes sense, whether an author has made a reasonable case for his or her claims. For example, Sophia, one of the authors in this book, tries to persuade you that a reading from coffee grounds is a valid way to learn about people and their futures. You can use hypothetical reasoning to decide whether she has made a reasonable argument supporting this idea. (Keep in mind that hypothetical reasoning will not necessarily prove that an author's claims are true—only whether the author has made a reasonable case for those claims. By determining this, you know whether the arguments are worth considering when you are deciding whether fortune-telling is real.)

To use hypothetical reasoning to analyze an article, you will use five steps:

1. State the author's claim (the hypothesis).
2. Gather the author's evidence supporting the claim.

3. Examine the author's evidence.

4. Consider alternative hypotheses, or explanations, for the evidence.

5. Draw a conclusion about the author's claim.

Using hypothetical reasoning to examine several articles about fortune-telling can give you a better perspective on the topic. You will begin to discern the difference between strong and weak evidence and to see which point of view has the most—or the best—supporting evidence.

The following sections demonstrate how to use hypothetical reasoning to critically examine some of the articles in this book. You can practice applying the method to other articles.

Step 1: State the Author's Claim

A hypothesis is the author's claim—the main idea the author of a persuasive article is trying to get the reader to accept; it is a factual statement that can be tested to determine the likelihood of its truth. In other words, it is not merely someone's opinion; by testing it, the reader can decide if it is true or false. To evaluate an article critically, start by stating the author's claim. This will be the hypothesis you are going to test as you critically examine the article. The author may make several claims. To simplify, here are sample claims for several of the articles in this book:

Author	Hypothesis
Raymond Buckland	Fortune-telling has survived for eons because it gets results.
Cassandra Eason	Fortune-telling helps people make wise decisions.
Morwyn	Fortune-tellers' insights come from many sources.
Jenni Kosarin	
J. Rainsnow	
Sophia	Coffee grounds reveal the future.

Author	Hypothesis
Katy Yocum	Fortune-telling is fake.
Mark Patrick Hederman	Tarot cards do not tell the future.
May Chow	Fortune-tellers are crooks.
Dougall Fraser	
The Straight Dope Science Advisory Board	
Michael Shermer	Palm-reading is not valid.

One important thing to remember when you write a hypothesis is that it should be a factual statement that is clear, specific, and provable. Look at the third hypothesis in the table above: "Fortune-tellers' insights come from many sources." This statement is quite general. It is better to make the hypothesis more specific. For example, this hypothesis could be changed to "Some fortune-tellers' insights are inspired by divine revelation." This is a narrower topic and is therefore easier to examine critically. Are there other hypotheses in the table above that you could make more specific?

When you determine the author's hypothesis, beware of drawing a conclusion the author did not intend. For example, as you read the article by May Chow, you must consider whether she is suggesting that all fortune-tellers are crooks or just the particular fortune-teller she focuses on.

Note that not every article has a provable hypothesis. If an article is purely a writer's opinion, you may not be able to state a provable hypothesis because an opinion is neither true nor false; it is simply what someone believes. Likewise, some authors avoid stating any clear claim. For example, many reporters remain as objective as possible, simply reporting what others say. Often, they report on two or more sides of an issue. You may not be able to write a provable hypothesis for such an article.

In the table above, four hypothesis spaces have been left empty. Write a clear, specific, and provable hypothesis for each of these four articles.

Step 2: Gather the Author's Evidence Supporting the Claim

Once you have a hypothesis, you must gather the evidence the author uses to support that claim. The evidence is everything the author uses to prove that his or her hypothesis is true. Sometimes an individual sentence is a piece of evidence. Sometimes a string of paragraphs or a section of the article is a piece of evidence. Let's look at the article by Sophia to see what kinds of evidence she uses to support her claim that coffee grounds can reveal the future. Here is some of her evidence:

1. The author states that reading coffee grounds is an art that has been passed down by an oral tradition.

2. The author reports that people have been reading coffee grounds since at least AD 1000.

3. The author argues that coffee grounds give better information than tea leaves.

4. The author states that the grounds in an empty coffee cup have a meaning and resemble symbols for each individual.

5. The author explains that the key skill in fortune-telling is to look at the psychic picture as a whole.

6. The author states that it is necessary to be able to separate fact from fantasy, which can be difficult.

7. The author states that what you see is important; what you expect doesn't matter.

Step 3: Examine the Evidence the Author Uses to Support the Claim

An author might use many types of evidence to support his or her claim. It is important to recognize different types of evidence and to evaluate whether they actually support the author's claim. Sophia uses unsupported statements of fact (items 1 and 4), statements of fact (item 2), statements of opinion (items 3 and 7), and appeals to reason (items 5 and 6).

Unsupported statements of fact (items 1 and 4). Sophia does not cite expert or eyewitness testimony in support of claims 1 and 4. Statements of fact do not need to be supported by testimony when they are widely considered to be common knowledge. Common knowledge does not necessarily mean that everyone can be expected to know it. Rather, a fact is considered common knowledge when so many experts have vouched for the fact that it is impractical to cite them all. Sophia might assume that some of her ideas are common knowledge. Are they? To find out for sure, it is necessary to do some research to discover whether these statements are widely accepted. Peforming some additional research would assist in evaluating her statements.

The practice of reading coffee grounds is not as common as other fortune-telling techniques. It is important to have critical thinking skills when evaluating the evidence. This is an area that might be difficult to test in a scientific setting, so much of your evidence will come from subjective accounts, not objective test results. Subjective accounts are prone to emotions and opinions, which further complicates the evidence.

Statements of fact (item 2). A statement of fact should present verifiable information—that is, it can be proven to be true or false. "A Baltimore oriole has orange feathers" is a statement of fact. You can find out if it is a true statement by looking in a book about birds. Most authors make many statements of fact, but not all of them are as easy to verify as the statement about the Baltimore oriole. For example, item 2, "people have been reading coffee grounds since at least A.D. 1000," could be very difficult to verify. To know that it is true, you would need specific information showing proof.

Ideally, the author should provide some evidence for you. She might describe a number of cases in which reading coffee grounds was used, or she might provide a footnote that gives information about a scientific study, for example. But many authors simply expect the reader to take their word for it. If you trust the author's expert knowledge, you might accept her statements as fact. But be careful about accepting facts just because the author states them. If a statement is not easy to verify, look for corroborating evidence (evidence that helps confirm their truth), either in the article itself or in an outside source.

Look at item 2. Is this statement of fact easy to verify?

Statements of opinion (items 3 and 7). Unlike statements of fact, statements of opinion cannot be verified. They cannot be proven to be right or wrong. They are statements that a person believes at the time he or she is saying them. Although statements of opinion are not actual evidence, if you have a positive impression of the author, they may bear weight when you evaluate the author's argument.

Appeals to reason (items 5 and 6). At some point, most writers who want to persuade the reader of something appeal to reason, logic, or common sense. Taken at face value, item 6 seems to make sense. After all, most people think it is important to be able to separate fact from fiction. One common example is religion: Most religions are based on faith—a belief that a god exists even though no one can prove this with physical evidence.

However, when you are examining a persuasive article, beware of accepting too much on faith—or on the author's word. You must watch carefully for examples of logical fallacy.

Logic comes from the Greek word for *reason. Logical thinking* means to reason things out. (Hypothetical reasoning is a form of logical thinking.) A logical fallacy is when logical reasoning fails—you think you are reasoning logically, but you are not. For example, you might make an overgeneralization: You say, "I had my coffee grounds read once and everything the reader told me was wrong. Therefore, reading coffee grounds is not a valid practice." But one coffee grounds reading is not really enough to generalize about the whole field. (This would also hold true if your single coffee grounds reading turned out to be right and you decided that coffee grounds reading really works. One reading is not a big enough sample on which to base a sound judgment.) As you read, carefully examine the author's appeals to reason and decide if they really make sense.

Step 4: Consider Alternative Hypotheses

Once you have examined the types of evidence the author has provided and have considered how valuable the evidence is in supporting the author's claims, see whether the author has considered other possible explanations. If the author considers only one explanation for the evidence, he or she may be presenting a biased, or one-sided, view or may not have fully considered the issue.

Look at Sophia's article again. Does she consider any of the challenges to reading coffee grounds? Does she address any objections people make claiming that reading coffee grounds doesn't work? (Failing to consider alternatives does not automatically invalidate a hypothesis, but it is one factor to consider.)

Step 5: Draw a Conclusion About the Author's Claim

After considering the evidence and alternative explanations, it is time to make a judgment, to decide whether the author's hypothesis makes sense. You can tally up the evidence that does and does not support the hypothesis and see how many pros and cons you have. But that is really too simple. You will have to give more weight to some evidence than to others.

Look again at Sophia's evidence. Which items do you find most important in support of reading coffee grounds? Which items do you consider unimportant? Decide: Do you think Sophia made a strong case for her hypothesis? Do you agree with her?

Exploring Further

Let's examine another article using hypothetical reasoning. Take a look at Michael Shermer's article, "Palm Reading Is Bunk." The first thing to look at is the author. The thing that stands out in the information preceding the article is that he is founder of the Skeptics Society, the editor of *Skeptic* magazine, and the author of several books with *skeptic* in the title. These facts suggest that Shermer probably has a bias against palmistry. However, he is also identified as a science writer. This means that if he is taking a scientific approach to the subject, he should examine it reasonably, looking for evidence on both sides of the question. In addition, the experiment takes place on a public television science show. Many people hold public television in high regard, so for them, this venue would lend credibility to the experiment and to Shermer. As you read, consider the following: Does Shermer seem unbiased, or does he unfairly stack the deck against palmistry?

Now, let's review Shermer's article using the steps for hypothetical reasoning.

Step 1: State a Hypothesis. Palmistry is not valid.

Step 2: Gather the Author's Evidence. Here is some of Shermer's evidence:

1. Shermer's main evidence is the experiment he conducts in which he pretends to be a palm reader.

2. The author states that psychic readings are "a form of improvisational acting."
3. The author says he planned some "useful nonsense" and threw in some "high-probability guesses" to tell his subject (client).
4. The author states that the subject assessed his reading positively, meaning that she thought it had some value or truth to it.
5. The author notes that he is not psychic and does not believe in extrasensory perception, or the ability to "read" another person's mind, or other psychic abilities.
6. The author posits that "there is not a shred of evidence that any of this is real."
7. The author argues that with some practice, he is certain he could host a successful psychic-reading television program and earn a lot of money. (In other words, anyone could conduct successful psychic readings even though they have no psychic ability.)
8. But, he adds, this would be wrong. In fact, it would be wantonly depraved to do so, he argues.
9. The author says that he "cannot imagine anything more insulting to the dead, and more insidious to the living, than constructing a fantasy that [the dead] are hovering nearby in the psychic aether, awaiting some self-proclaimed psychic conduit to reveal . . . breathtaking insights."

Step 3: Examine the Evidence. In this article, Shermer relies most heavily on his scientific experiment to support his hypothesis. He also uses ridicule, name-calling, and innuendo (items 2, 3, and 9); statements of fact (items 4); statements of opinion (items 5, 6, and 7); and loaded words and appeals to emotion (items 8 and 9).

Experiment. Experiments, if conducted in a controlled, scientific manner, can provide excellent evidence to prove or disprove a hypothesis. In fact, hypothetical reasoning and scientific experimenting are very similar. Both have a hypothesis, and both attempt to prove or disprove the hypothesis. In a scientific experiment, the scientist sets up conditions or tests that can be carefully monitored, then analyzes the results. To be considered valid, the experiments must be able to be repeated with the same results.

Shermer's experiment is designed to test the hypothesis that a phony palmist (himself) can convince people that his palmistry is genuine. You, the reader, must decide if Shermer's experiment is set up in a scientific way and if its results bolster his hypothesis.

Ridicule, name-calling, and innuendo (items 2, 3 and 9). Ridicule, name-calling, and innuendo make fun of something or demean it in order to decrease its credibility. Ridicule and name-calling may be very apparent; innuendo is more subtle— the person who uses innuendo merely implies something rather than states it openly. For example, in the last paragraph of the article, where Shermer writes that he could not make money by pretending to be a psychic because of his "evolved moral sentiments and guilt-laden scruples," he is implying that fortune-tellers are immoral and unscrupulous, even though he does not say that directly.

In general, using tactics of ridicule, name-calling, and innuendo is not useful evidence. Many times, an author uses these as a substitute for real evidence. You must read carefully to see if there is any evidence behind them.

Look at items 2, 3, and 9. For which items has the author provided some supporting evidence?

Statements of fact (item 4). Review the information about statements of fact earlier in this chapter. Then decide if item 4 provides good evidence for Shermer's hypothesis.

Statements of opinion (items 5, 6, and 7). Unlike statements of fact, statements of opinion cannot be verified. They cannot be proven to be right or wrong. They are what someone believes about something. Although they are not actual evidence, if you have a positive impression of the author, they may bear weight when you evaluate the author's argument.

Loaded words and appeals to emotion (items 8 and 9). Loaded words are words that have strong feelings attached to them. For instance, many people have strong feelings about their country, so an author may try to make you think that his argument is patriotic. Many authors like to appeal to emotion because it can be a good way to get you on their side. In the last paragraph of Shermer's article, he makes strong appeals to the reader's emotions. "Wantonly depraved" is a very emotion-laden phrase; naturally, if the opposite point of view is wantonly depraved, no reasonable person would want to have anything to do with it. And when Shermer writes about insulting the dead, he knows that most people have some dear relatives or friends who are dead and whom you certainly would not want to insult.

Beware of appeals to emotion. An argument that relies on emotion is not necessarily wrong, but emotion can easily blind you to reason.

Step 4: Consider Alternative Hypotheses. Does Shermer consider alternative hypotheses? Can you think of alternative hypotheses he should have considered?

Step 5: Draw a Conclusion. You decide: Does Shermer make a good case for palmistry being a fraud? What evidence most influences your decision?

Other Evidence

Authors use various kinds of evidence to support their arguments in addition to the types mentioned above. Two very common ones are eyewitness reports and statistics.

Eyewitness testimony. When dealing with controversial topics, an author often will use eyewitness testimony, or first-person accounts. For example, some of the articles in this book describe a person's experience with a fortune-teller. To some people, accounts like these are enough to convince them that fortune-telling is (or is not) real. But a scientist would examine these accounts carefully because eyewitness testimony and personal accounts are notoriously unreliable.

Perhaps you know about the eyewitness experiment in which people are sitting in a classroom listening to a lecture or doing some other activity. Suddenly, the classroom door bursts open, and a stranger enters. The stranger may "rob" one of the witnesses or do something else dramatic. Then the stranger leaves.

A few moments later, the instructor asks the students to tell what they witnessed. Invariably, different students remember different things. One remembers that the stranger was of average height and weight; another remembers that he was thin or heavy. One remembers that he had red hair; another remembers that a hood covered the stranger's head. One remembers that he was carrying a weapon; another remembers that his hands were empty. And so on.

When something unexpected happens, especially when it happens quickly or when it evinces great emotion, the mind is not prepared to remember details. Even when the event is expected, the witness can see things differently than what actually happened. This unreliability has many causes: Some people simply are not good observers. Others have preconceived ideas that influence their observation: They believe that robbers are male, so when they see a robber whose features aren't very clear, they assume the person must be male. Some people have recently experienced something that influences what they see. For example, if you have just come home from a scary movie, hearing an unusual sound in your house can make you certain you are about to be set upon by a monster or a serial killer. People may go to a palm reader already believing in palmistry, or they may go to a fortune-teller desperate to find advice that will help them make a decision, or they may go believing that fortune-telling is merely a game and cannot provide anything of real value. An additional factor is that a single person's experience may not give a broad enough picture of a subject to judge it fairly.

For all these reasons and more, you have to be very careful about accepting eyewitness testimony and personal accounts as the main kind of evidence. This is why in crime investigations, for example, the police often try to find independent corroborating witnesses—several people who saw the same event and have not spoken with each other so that their accounts have not been influenced by anyone else's version. If two or more witnesses independently report the same details, the chances are better that the details are accurate.

When an author uses an eyewitness report or personal account, look for other evidence in the article that helps support it.

Statistics. Authors sometimes use statistics or other numerical data to support their claims or to refute their opponents' claims. For example, they may state that an idea is correct because of the large number of people who believe it. When deciding whether something happened by chance or on purpose, statistics can be very important. But be sure to evaluate all numerical claims carefully. Where did the numbers come from? If they are from a survey, how old is the survey? What do the numbers really mean?

Now You Do It!

Choose one article from this book that has not already been analyzed and use hypothetical reasoning to determine if the author's evidence supports the hypothesis. Here is a form you can use:

Name of article_____   Author_____

1. State the author's hypothesis.
2. List the evidence.

3. Examine the evidence. For each item of evidence listed, state what type of evidence it is (statement of fact, appeal to reason, etc.) and evaluate it: Does it appear to be valid evidence? Does it appear to support the author's hypothesis?

4. Consider alternative hypotheses. What alternative hypotheses does the author consider? Does he or she consider them fairly? If the author rejects them, does the rejection seem reasonable? Are there other alternative explanations you believe should be considered? Explain.

5. Draw a conclusion about the hypothesis. Does the author adequately support his or her claim? Do you believe the author's hypothesis is valid? Explain.

For Further Research

Books

Raymond Buckland, *The Fortune-Telling Book: The Encyclopedia of Divination and Soothsaying.* Canton, MI: Visible Ink, 2004.

Raymond Buckland, *Secrets of Gypsy Fortunetelling.* St. Paul: Llewellyn, 1988.

Scott Cunningham, *Divination for Beginners: Reading the Past, Present & Future.* St. Paul: Llewellyn, 2001.

Cassandra Eason, *The Complete Guide to Divination: How to Foretell the Future Using the Most Popular Methods of Prediction.* Berkeley, CA: Crossing, 2003.

Ann Fiery, *The Book of Divination.* San Francisco: Chronicle, 1999.

Dougall Fraser, *But You Knew That Already: What a Psychic Can Teach You About Life.* Emmaus, PA: Rodale, 2005.

Judy Hall, *What Does My Future Hold? 99 Ways to Plan Your Life.* New York: Penguin/Compass, 2001.

Paul Halpern, *The Pursuit of Destiny: A History of Prediction.* Cambridge, MA: Perseus, 2000.

Mark Patrick Hederman, *Tarot: Talisman or Taboo?* Blackrock, Ireland: Currach, 2003.

William W. Hewitt, *Tea Leaf Reading.* St. Paul: Llewellyn, 1989.

P. Scott Hollander, *Tarot for Beginners.* St. Paul: Llewellyn, 1995.

Terry Iacuzzo, *Small Mediums at Large: The True Tale of a Family of Psychics.* New York: Perigee/Berkeley/Penguin, 2004.

Lynne Kelly, *The Skeptic's Guide to the Paranormal.* New York: Thunder's Mouth, 2004.

Jenni Kosarin, *The Everything Divining the Future Book.* Avon, MA: Adams Media, 2003.

John Matthews, ed. *The World Atlas of Divination: Systems of Divining the Future and How They Are Used Around the World.* London: Headline, 1994.

Donna McCue with Stacey Donovan, *Your Fate Is in Your Hands: Using the Principles of Palmistry to Change Your Life.* New York: Pocket, 2000.

Mark McElroy, *Putting the Tarot to Work.* St. Paul: Llewellyn, 2004.

Morwyn, *The Complete Book of Psychic Arts.* St. Paul: Llewellyn, 1999.

Clifford Pickover, *Dreaming the Future: The Fantastic Story of Prediction.* Amherst, NY: Prometheus, 2001.

Dean Radin, *The Conscious Universe: The Scientific Truth of Psychic Phenomena.* San Francisco: HarperEdge, 1997.

James Randi, *Flim-Flam!* Buffalo, NY: Prometheus, 1982.

Sophia, *Fortune in a Coffee Cup: Divination with Coffee Grounds.* St. Paul: Llewellyn Worldwide, 1999.

Sophia, *Fortune Telling with Playing Cards.* St. Paul: Llewellyn, 1998.

Robert A. Steiner, *Don't Get Taken! Bunco and Bunkum Exposed: How to Protect Yourself.* El Cerrito, CA: Wide-Awake, 1989.

Jane Struthers, *The Palmistry Bible.* New York: Sterling, 2005.

Richard Williams, ed. *Quest for the Unknown: Charting the Future.* Pleasantville, NY: Reader's Digest, 1992.

Periodicals

Michael E. Bakich, "Astrology: Fact or Fiction?" *Astronomy*, vol. 32, no. 12, December 2004.

William J. Broad, "For Delphic Oracle, Fumes and Visions," *New York Times*, March 19, 2002.

May Chow, "Psychic Scams," *Asian Week*, April 25, 2003.

Miranda Fettes, "In Touch with the Spiritual," *Evening News* (Edinburgh), June 17, 2002.

Stephen Glass, "Prophets and Losses: The Futures Market for Phone Psychics," *Harper's*, February 1998.

Ray Hyman, "Guide to Cold Reading: How to Convince Strangers That You Know All About Them," *Skeptical Inquirer*, Spring/Summer 1977.

Jonathan Leake, "Top Scientist Gives Backing to Astrology," *Sunday Times* (London), May 16, 2004.

Leah McLaren, "Seeing Things: A Psychic Explosion Is in the Cards," *Globe & Mail* (Toronto), September 4, 1999.

Michael Shermer, "Psychic for a Day," *Skeptic*, vol. 10, no. 1, 2003.

Joshua Tompkins, "Who Invented the Fortune Cookie?" *American Heritage*, February-March 2005.

Katy Yocum, "A Reading Between the Lines," *Louisville Magazine*, July 2001.

Alex Williams, "Hooked on Online Psychics," *New York Times*, March 5, 2006.

Index